MANAGERS'
FIRST AID
KIT

MANAGERS'
FIRST AID
KIT

—— A PRACTICAL GUIDE TO ——
REMEDY THE THREE MOST COMMON
MANAGERIAL CHALLENGES

JOAN H. UNDERWOOD

UTDS
PUBLISHING
under-exient Talent Development Services

St. Michael, Barbados

MANAGERS' FIRST AID KIT:
A PRACTICAL GUIDE TO REMEDY THE THREE MOST
COMMON MANAGERIAL CHALLENGES

The information provided within this book is for general informational and educational purposes only. The author makes no representations or warranties, express or implied, about the completeness, accuracy, reliability, suitability or availability with respect to the information, products, services, or related graphics contained in this book for any purpose. Any use of this information is at your own risk.

MANAGERS' FIRST AID KIT: A PRACTICAL GUIDE TO REMEDY
THE THREE MOST COMMON MANAGERIAL CHALLENGES
© 2020 Joan H. Underwood

Paperback ISBN-13: 978-976-96517-0-8
Paperback Premium Edition ISBN-13: 978-976-96517-1-5

Published by Underwood Talent Development Services (UTDS) Publishing
St. Michael, Barbados

Printed in Barbados
First Edition October 2020

Cover and Interior Design by: Make Your Mark Publishing Solutions
Editing by: Make Your Mark Publishing Solutions

CONTENTS

PART III: MANAGING SYSTEMS & PROCESSES

PART IV: EPILOGUE

ACKNOWLEDGEMENTS

THIS BOOK IS A LABOUR OF LOVE AND A TOKEN OF MY APPRECIA-tion for the individuals and teams that I've had the privilege to lead over the past thirty years. While I held the pen on the manuscript, the final product is inarguably a team effort. I take the opportunity here to acknowledge those who played a pivotal role in that team.

I must begin with my husband, Rudie—the yang to my ying. Thank you for being such a source of love, joy, and music in my life, and for teaching me the importance of balance and harmony.

The second most instrumental person on this project has been my niece Carissa. The book is dedicated to you, Cris; each chapter was written with you in mind, with a view to helping you attain even higher levels of professional success.

The next most important contribution to this manuscript came from Christopher Wrenn, who diligently reviewed each chapter and challenged both my thinking and my writing, thereby helping to bring greater clarity and structure to the book. However, the greatest gift you gave me was that of taking the time to understand and appreciate my vision for this project. I look forward to collaborating with you again in the future.

My love and thanks go out to Brendalie Josiah, Blanka Charles, Oneka Martin-Bird, Kerry Willock, Patsy Richards, and Emarline Thomas for giving me permission to share our stories, and for the love and support you've given me both on and off the job. I've learnt so much from each of you. You've helped me to become not just a better leader, but a better person.

To my friend, colleague, and mentor Lisa James, I extend appreciation for taking the time to review the latter chapters. As always, your feedback was insightful, and your encouragement was a source of inspiration for me.

Thank you as well to my peer coaches—Marjorie and Sonia. Our Friday evening sessions were often a welcome oasis after a challenging work week. My interactions with you cause me to think deeply and to truly believe that the work we do positively impacts the lives of others.

In closing, I give thanks to God, and stand firm on the promise that I can do all things through Christ who strengthens me.

For Carissa
You inspire me.

Joan H Underwood

AUTHOR

INTRODUCTION

OVER TWO DECADES AGO, I KNEW A YOUNG WAITRESS—LET'S CALL her Lydia—who had the enviable knack of making each guest in the all-inclusive hotel where she worked feel that they were the most important person in the room. Guests frequently mentioned Lydia by name when completing their customer feedback forms, and repeat visitors were excited to see her smiling face and incredulous that she remembered their names. It wasn't just guests who appreciated Lydia and her work ethic. Management knew they could always rely on her to go the extra mile to ensure guests had a memorable holiday experience.

Then one day, management decided to reward Lydia's exceptional performance by promoting her to the position of maitre d'. Everyone was so happy for her. She was delighted that management valued her contribution to the hotel's success. Of course, the extra income was great too.

But everything didn't exactly go as planned. Whenever the restaurant got busy, instead of planning, leading, and organising (managerial functions), Lydia reverted to what came most naturally to her. In other words, she reverted to carrying out the functions of a waitress. This left the members of her team scurrying around on their own, and created the impression that no one was in control.

After a few months, management was disappointed; Lydia was demoralised; and the other members of the team missed the smiling, friendly, outgoing coworker they had grown to know and love.

It was Lydia and so many other good people who share her experience who motivated me to write this book. Far too often employers reward employees for doing a good job as an individual contributor by promoting them to a supervisory or managerial position. Unfortunately, they do so without helping those high-performing employees to acquire and/or develop the knowledge, skills, and abilities they need to succeed in their new role. As a result, high performers such as Lydia may experience feelings of frustration, and even fail in the new role.

Research published by The Ken Blanchard Companies® revealed that new managers are not getting the training they need to succeed. As a result, 51% of the managers in that study reported that they felt unprepared for their new role. The findings of that study were not an isolated event. Research from CEB revealed that as many as 60% of new managers either underperformed or failed in their first two years.

I conceptualised this book as a first aid kit for people like Lydia and the 51% of respondents in the study published by The Ken Blanchard Companies. It's also for all those who can relate to the 53% of newly appointed managers who told Officevibe that they didn't have an accurate understanding of what it meant to be a manager when they took up the position.

The American College of Emergency Physicians recommends that each household have a first aid kit packed with supplies and equipment to correct minor problems and prevent them from becoming big problems which require a major intervention—such as a trip to the hospital. In much the same way, I've written this book with the intention that new and aspiring managers will use it as their first resource to help them successfully transition to their new role. By following this practical guide, new managers reduce the likelihood of falling prey to the most common pitfalls such as those experienced by Lydia.

With this book, you have access to a guide to help you anticipate and skilfully navigate the challenges you will inevitably encounter. In a 2013 *Harvard Business Review* article titled "The Focused Leader," Daniel Goleman posited that every leader needs to cultivate three levels of focus—inward focus, focus on others, and outward focus. That paradigm aligns with the design of this book, in that it has been structured around three levels of managerial challenges—managing self, managing others, and managing systems and processes.

As someone who has been certified as a Senior Professional in Human Resources (SPHR) for over a decade, and who is a designated Master Trainer and certified Professional Coach, I have amassed a wealth of experience and had a first-hand view of the highs and lows experienced by new managers. Additionally, based on my experience as a subject matter expert and graduate-level lecturer and facilitator with the Cave Hill School of Business at the University of the West Indies, I know that traditional business school text books are not as accessible, and do not necessarily provide the practical support new managers need.

Many of the personal experiences I share in this book came from my time on what, to date, is still the most high-performing team I've had the privilege to lead or observe at work—the HR Department at ABI Holdings Ltd. Those ladies continue to inspire me with their professionalism, as well as their individual and collective strength, authenticity, and ability to get the job done. I share our stories with their permission and with the hope that they will help you with your personal journey.

I begin the book with a focus on self as I define emotional intelligence—which, according to Warren Bennis, can account for up to 85 to 90% of success at work. I then go on to draw on the work of Dr. Susan David to share how you can develop emotional agility so that you choose how to respond rather than being hijacked by your emotions—or the emotions or actions of those around you. The rest of Part I contains other essential gems such as cultivating winning habits, making the distinction between blame and accountability, and choosing your attitude. I then close out the Managing Self section of the book by examining what is arguably the most important issue—i.e. self-care.

In Part II, the focus shifts to managing others. That discussion begins with trust and goes on to cover the other essential building blocks for mutually beneficial working relationships. In keeping with my commitment to be your guide on the side, I go on to provide strategies and proven tips on the essentials, such as giving and receiving feedback, effective delegation, and managing your boss.

In Part III, attention shifts to the processes and systems that will determine your level of efficiency. You will discover what is required to create and sustain a high-performance team, to coach your direct reports in a way that will optimise their performance, and to conduct great meetings. One of the keys to creating and maintaining a high-performance team is understanding each of your direct report's preferred role within the team. As a special bonus for purchasing this book, you are entitled to a 40% discount on the purchase of a Belbin's Individual Report.

Your Belbin Individual Report will be generated following your online completion of the proprietary assessment, which identifies the combination of the nine Belbin Team Roles you exhibit, and gives you advice on how to use your Team Role strengths in the workplace. To access your discount, simply visit https://www.belbin. com/belbin-for-individuals/belbin-individual-reports/ and enter the code UTDS40JK. My thanks go out to Jo Keeler and the rest of the team at Belbin Associates for their generosity in extending this offer to my readers.

Throughout each section of the book, you will find questions to take you through guided introspection as well as activities that will help you apply the lessons learnt in real time. I strongly encourage you to complete these exercises and activities. Research has shown that we best learn by doing. Or, as the Chinese philosopher Xun Kuang reportedly said, "Tell me and I forget, teach me and I may remember, involve me and I learn."

I'm a big proponent of the importance of choices in life. Therefore, I exhort you to choose carefully what seeds you plant while on your journey to becoming the best manager you could possibly be. I hope that this poem will serve to inspire you to make good choices each and every day so that you will, in due course, reap the benefits of those choices.

> *If you plant honesty, you will reap trust.*
> *If you plant goodness, you will reap friends.*
> *If you plant humility, you will reap greatness.*
> *If you plant perseverance, you will reap contentment.*
> *If you plant consideration, you will reap perspective.*
> *If you plant hard work, you will reap success.*
> *If you plant forgiveness, you will reap reconciliation.*
> *So, be careful what you plant now.*
> *It will determine what you will reap later.*
>
> Author Unknown

PART I
MANAGING SELF

CHAPTER ONE

EMOTIONAL INTELLIGENCE

"Success in the knowledge economy comes to those who know themselves–their strengths, their values, and how they best perform."
–Peter F Drucker

M ANAGING OTHERS IS THE MOST CHALLENGING AND YET POTEN-tially the most rewarding role that you can assume—unless, of course, you're a parent. That trumps everything! In fact, the two roles tend to elicit similar emotions. Both new parents and new managers often find their new role somewhat intimidating. The ones who don't are probably underestimating the magnitude of the challenges ahead. So, if you're feeling a tad overwhelmed, I hope you derive some measure of comfort from knowing that you're not alone, but more importantly, I want to assure you that challenging is not synonymous with impossible.

I absolutely adore the 5 P's motto, which states *proper preparation prevents poor performance.* Preparation is key to positioning yourself to succeed in your role as manager. While your intelligence and/

or technical skills got you to this point, in order to succeed going forward, there's something else that you simply must have in your toolkit—emotional intelligence (EI).

There is no shortage of definitions for EI. However, for our purposes, we will define it as an individual's ability to be aware of, control, and express their emotions, and to handle interpersonal relationships judiciously and empathetically. That's quite a lot to take in. So let's spend some time examining each of these components.

Self-Awareness

We are sometimes quite taken aback by the impression that others have of us. Perhaps there have been instances when, based on conclusions that others have drawn about you, you thought, *They don't know me at all!* The truth is that there are things about yourself that you just don't know. You're not alone. We all have blind spots.

Back in 1955, psychologists Joseph Luft and Harry Ingham developed a model to capture the different levels of self-awareness. In time, it became known as the Johari Window[1]—a play on the first names of the two developers.

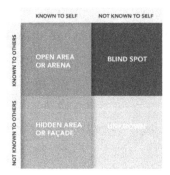

THE JOHARI WINDOW MODEL

[1] https://www.selfawareness.org.uk/news/understanding-the-johari-window-model

JOAN H. UNDERWOOD

No matter how well you think you know yourself, there are things about you that you simply don't know, but which are apparent to those who interact with you. This is really important, because if you don't know something, you can't manage it. The good news is that you can bring information from your blind spot into the open area, thereby giving you a higher level of self-awareness. And while self-awareness doesn't guarantee wisdom, it certainly is a precursor to it.

I'll use a personal example to illustrate how information can move between quadrants in the Johari Window. Several years ago, I was managing a very high-performance team when the performance level of one of the team members took a downward turn. She started to miss deadlines, and the quality of her work showed signs of slipping. When I inquired about what was happening, she was very apologetic but offered no explanation.

As the sub-optimal performance persisted, I grew impatient. I had come to expect the team to function like a well-oiled machine and was frustrated that that was no longer the case. I should point out here that, by regular standards, the team was still delivering the goods.

Then one day, three other team members came to my office and asked if they could speak with me. The fact that they closed the door behind them alerted me that this was serious. They were respectful but resolute as they told me my impatience with our colleague was showing and it was having an adverse impact on the team's morale. They went on to acknowledge that her performance had slipped, and while they indicated they were prepared to help pick up the slack, they needed me to be more empathetic since she was struggling with a personal issue.

Until the 'intervention,' I had no idea that my own behaviour was more problematic than my direct report's temporary dip in performance. Once this information moved from my blind spot to my open area, I was able to apologise and take corrective measures.

There are a couple of channels you can pursue to develop greater self-awareness. Since, by definition, the information in your blind spot is known to others, you could simply ask for feedback from those with whom you interact. That requires a certain willingness to be vulnerable. And vulnerability requires trust—the conviction that the other person has your best interests at heart and means you no harm.

In the story I just shared, because my team had built up a strong repository of trust, my direct reports thought it would be safe to provide me with feedback and that I would give serious consideration to what they had to say.

In any event, this type of feedback is simply information—information about how others perceive you. What you choose to do with that feedback is completely up to you. My suggestion is that you view it as a gift. Whether or not you agree with the information others provide, it's a gift in that you now have something you didn't have before—i.e. insight to what others are thinking and the stories they're telling themselves about you. Once you know those stories, you have an opportunity to take steps to change the narrative.[2]

Another way you can increase your self-awareness is by completing a scientifically validated psychometric assessment. Such assessment tools analyse information you provide to draw certain conclusions about your personality, behaviours, and preferences.[i]

Self-Management

Having become aware of the information that was previously in your blind spot, you now have the opportunity to manage those

---

[2] For more information on changing the narrative, please see Chapter 12 on Giving and Receiving Feedback.

JOAN H. UNDERWOOD

habits, behaviours, emotions, traits, etc., to create the outcomes you desire. Among the things you need to decide is whether the newly revealed habit or behaviour helps or hinders the pursuit of your goals. Ultimately you want to eliminate any and all self-defeating actions, and to maintain and reinforce those which align well with your goals.

It is important to understand and appreciate that there is nothing inherently bad about any emotion. Rather, what determines the outcome is how you express your emotions. Emotions such as anger and irritation can serve as a force for good once properly channelled. That is the domain of emotional self-regulation.

Emotional self-regulation or management is the ability to express your emotions in a manner that is socially acceptable and compatible with your desired outcomes. This requires the ability to determine when it is appropriate to act spontaneously as well as the ability to defer your response.

Let's imagine for a moment that you're prone to expressing irritation by raising your voice or using biting sarcasm. Think about the impact that could have on the various members of your team. While some team members might just go with the flow, others could find it quite intimidating. As a result, they might conclude that you're unapproachable or moody or some other more colourful but less complimentary adjective. In any event, the potential downside is significant.

Back in 2009, the general elections in the Caribbean nation of Antigua and Barbuda attracted international attention when several of the polling stations failed to open on time. Some opened as late as six hours after the scheduled start of voting. I was subsequently commissioned by the Commonwealth Secretariat[3][ii] to prepare a case study geared towards extracting the leadership lessons from what had been dubbed the General Elections Fiasco.

---

[3] http://utdsinc.com/deconstructing-the-2009-general-elections-in-antigua-and-barbuda-a-case-study/

My research revealed that a printer had malfunctioned on the eve of the general elections, thereby delaying the printing of certain documents that were required to commence voting. The officer in charge did not escalate the matter to the Supervisor of Elections, but rather tried unsuccessfully to resolve the situation on her own.

Upon reporting for duty a few hours ahead of the scheduled opening of the polling stations, the Supervisor of Elections realised what had transpired. She immediately sprang into action doing all within her power to resolve the problem. Notably, however, she did not refer the matter to the Chairman of the Electoral Commission or the Prime Minister, both of whom would have been able to access additional resources in the quest to rectify the problem.

During my interview with her, the Supervisor of Elections identified her direct report's failure to notify her of the problem with the printer as a critical inflection point. However, she did not consider her own failure to escalate the matter as a contributory factor.

Whether consciously or subconsciously, we convey messages to others about how we are likely to respond to bad news. Those messages have implications for the performance of your department and possibly the entire organisation. In the case of the 2009 General Elections Fiasco in Antigua and Barbuda, the dominant organisational culture was one which did not encourage staff to report bad news up the chain of command. As a result, the full range of available resources was not deployed to resolve the problem.

Here's something for you to think about—you cannot not communicate! Whether you use words or not, whether you're conscious of it or not, you are always communicating. Your staff or direct reports look to you for both verbal and non-verbal cues. In their eyes, you cast a long shadow. Your behaviour and moods set the tone. In fact, you should consider them as being contagious.

People above you in the chain of command are also paying

JOAN H. UNDERWOOD

attention to you and how you express yourself. Such individuals look to you to assess how effectively you're communicating organisational plans and policies to your team. So, please bear in mind that even your silence is communication that will be interpreted by others.

One of the skills you need to develop is the ability to ensure that the messages you communicate are well aligned to your intentions. This means you need to master subtleties such as body language, tone of voice, facial expressions, etc. Unless you've received feedback on this before, chances are you are not fully aware of how you're managing this type of communication. So, one of your first orders of business should be to find people you trust and request that they give you candid feedback.

After you get that feedback, you then need to determine if it's working for you. If so, great! Continue reading to get insights on how you can build on that success. If not, continue reading to find out how you can turn that around and become a more effective and powerful communicator.

It is particularly important for supervisors and managers to master the spectrum of aggression, assertiveness, and submissiveness. While there will always be a certain level of subjectivity associated with how people characterise your placement on this spectrum, there are some things you should keep in mind.

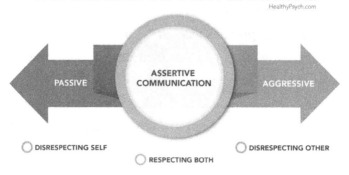

THE COMMUNICATION SPECTRUM

HealthyPsych.com

PASSIVE

ASSERTIVE COMMUNICATION

AGGRESSIVE

DISRESPECTING SELF

RESPECTING BOTH

DISRESPECTING OTHER

Let's start with a few working definitions. Assertiveness refers to your ability to express yourself in a manner that is self-assured and confident without infringing on the rights of others to do likewise. In contrast, aggression describes forceful action or speech, which serves to dominate or in some other way harm or constrain others. At the other extreme of this spectrum is submissiveness—a tendency to yield to the will of others even when doing so is detrimental to your own interests.

Think about where you fall on this spectrum. Think about where others such as your manager, peers, and direct reports would place you. I encourage you to be candid with yourself and to explore whether this could be a blind spot for you. If your current position on the spectrum is not in alignment with where you would like to be and how you would like to be perceived by others, throughout the book I will be outlining the steps necessary to get you there. The very first step is to take an audit of the quality of your interpersonal relationships.

Social Awareness

Social awareness is the ability to accurately pick up on emotions in other people, to understand what's going on with them, and to perceive what they are thinking and feeling. It is sometimes referred to as a person's ability to read a room. Empathy is at the heart of social awareness.

JOAN H. UNDERWOOD

Empathy is often confused with sympathy and compassion, which are generally about feeling sorry for someone, especially in the face of some type of misfortune. In contrast, empathy enables you to recognise, understand, and appreciate how other people feel. Instead of feeling sorry for the other person (as is the case with sympathy and compassion), with empathy, what you experience and express is understanding and respect. We will take a deeper dive into empathy in Chapter 9.

Social awareness also applies to your ability to understand organisational culture. This is a particularly important skill set for new managers, since you are required to successfully navigate the organisational culture. Your bosses expect you to champion and uphold the culture. Your direct reports look to you to lead by example. That's virtually impossible to do if you don't actually understand the culture and you lack organisational savvy, which starts with the ability to operate within the organisation's formal and informal structures and extends to the ability to build alliances. That brings us to the fourth component of emotional intelligence.

Interpersonal Relationships

In the context of EI, this refers to the extent you develop and maintain mutually beneficial relationships. It involves understanding and appreciating how others feel. Therefore, one of the hallmarks of successful interpersonal relationships is empathy. However, it extends beyond one-on-one relationships to include how you view society as a whole along with your roles and responsibilities within the society.

Trust is another fundamental building block of all good relationships—whether personal or professional. Conversely, a lack of trust is at the heart of almost all pathology that can be found in relationships and in entire organisations. You can spend years building up trust in a relationship. However, it can all be lost in an instant with a careless word or deed. Chapter 8 will help you avoid that pitfall.

As a manager, the success of your interpersonal relationships—whether they be with your direct reports, peers, bosses, clients, or other external stakeholders—will depend in large measure on your ability to find common ground, to build rapport, to persuade and influence, to resolve conflicts, and to inspire confidence in others. In the upcoming chapters, I will provide practical guidance on how you can develop these competencies.

 ## Self-Reflection Exercise: How Emotionally Intelligent Are You?

We've covered a lot of ground in this first chapter. It's useful to reflect on how this information has landed with you. The following questions are designed to do just that. I encourage you to take some time to think about your answers to these questions. You may also wish to start a journal or to record them on a device of your choice. As you continue your journey of learning and development, these exercises will help you track your progress and document your insights and breakthroughs.

1. Which of the elements of EI comes most naturally to you?
   A. Self-awareness
   B. Self-management
   C. Social Awareness
   D. Interpersonal relationships
2. Which of the elements of EI challenges you the most?
3. Based on what we have covered in this chapter, what is one thing that you would like to
   A. Start doing?
   B. Stop doing?
   C. Continue doing?

JOAN H. UNDERWOOD

CHAPTER TWO

EMOTIONAL AGILITY

"Effective leaders are mindful of their inner experiences but not caught in them."

–Susan David

L ET'S NOW TURN YOUR ATTENTION TO EMOTIONAL AGILITY. THIS term was coined by Dr. Susan David[4] [iii] to refer to the ability to manage your thoughts and feelings. Emotional Agility fits nicely in the space between self-awareness and self-expression. Leaders at all levels struggle to navigate that space. By reading this chapter, and applying the lessons learnt, you could be well on your way to self-mastery.

According to John Keyser,[5] [iv] emotional intelligence is more important for job performance than any other leadership skill. In fact, it is more than twice as important as our technical knowledge. The good news is that emotional intelligence can be developed. Throughout my personal journey, including my work as an

---

[4] https://hbr.org/2016/11/how-to-manage-your-emotions-without-fighting-them
[5] https://www.td.org/insights/emotional-intelligence-is-key-to-our-success

executive coach, I have come to the realization that self-awareness (a critical element of emotional intelligence) is the beginning of wisdom. However, it is just that—the beginning, and not the entire journey.

One of the critical factors in determining whether the journey ends at wisdom or some other less desirable destination is the choice that you make whether or not to express the emotions you experience. Further, having decided whether to express an emotion, it is also vital to decide how best to express the emotion to move closer to your desired outcomes. Both of those decisions fall within the purview of emotional agility.

Circumventing the Amygdala Hijack

I'm sure you can recall at least one incident when you reacted in a way that was driven purely by a fight, flight, or freeze instinct. You know what I mean—that experience where you acted in haste and then found yourself repenting at leisure. You're not alone in that regard. We've all experienced it.

That instinctive response is a holdover from the days when early humans were exposed to the constant threat of being killed or injured by wild animals or other tribes. The fight-or-flight response evolved as a survival mechanism—i.e. an automatic response to physical danger that allows you to react quickly without thinking. When you feel threatened and afraid, the amygdala automatically activates the fight-or-flight response by sending out signals to release stress hormones that prepare your body to fight or run away. In some instances, the instinctive response could also be to freeze. The fight, flight, or freeze responses are triggered by emotions like fear, anxiety, aggression, and anger.

JOAN H. UNDERWOOD

By developing your self-awareness and emotional agility, you can circumvent future hijacks. Fundamental to mastering your emotions is the realization that they are a resource for you rather than a force that is bigger than you are.

Holocaust survivor and author Viktor Frankl[6] [v] described the space between a stimulus and your response as where you have the power to choose. Instead of reacting by succumbing to the amygdala hijack, you can develop the capacity to mindfully insert your values and intentions into the space between the stimulus and your response, thereby choosing if and how to respond. Part of the mindful processing of stimuli is assessing if and how the contemplated response serves your greater purpose and/or values.

Here's the thing, though—to do so, you have to use a different part of your brain. Instead of leaving it up to your amygdala, emotional agility engages your cerebral cortex. This is the more evolved, rational part of your brain. This is where thinking, reasoning, decision-making, and planning take place.

Four Steps to Emotional Agility

Susan David outlines the following steps you can use to leverage your cerebral cortex and improve your emotional agility and, by extension, your personal efficacy:

1. Notice when you've been hooked or triggered by your thoughts and feelings.
2. Label your thoughts and emotions.
3. Accept your thoughts and emotions by acknowledging them and exploring them from a position of curiosity.
4. Act on your values.

---

[6] https://www.amazon.com/Mans-Search-Meaning-Viktor-Frankl/dp/1416524282

By inserting these steps in the space between experiencing a stimulus and reacting to it, you position yourself to become much more resourceful.

The reality is that all emotions—even the negative ones—have a positive intent. Once you identify that positive intent, you can then align your actions with it rather than with the negative emotion itself.

So, what might that look like in real life? Let's imagine that you're scheduled to make a big presentation at work and you're experiencing fear. What is the positive intent or value associated with fear? It might be the desire to impress your boss or prove that the company made the right decision in promoting you. Or maybe you see this as your opportunity to make the case that you are ready to take on a new and more challenging assignment. If you allow your amygdala to hijack the moment, you would probably freeze.

Alternatively, if you notice what you're experiencing—i.e. your physiological response—and then put the appropriate label on that response, the conversation in your mind might sound something like this:

- *My heart is racing right now, and I'm sweating even though the A/C is on full blast...*
- *I'm experiencing these feelings because I'm anxious...*
- *I'm anxious because the stakes are high, and I want to succeed*
- *What do I need to do now, and who do I need to be, in order to have the best possible outcome in this situation?*

Having had that conversation, you are now in the position to choose a response that is aligned with your values and intent, rather than simply defaulting to a reaction that could be irrational and/or destructive.

JOAN H. UNDERWOOD

Reaction versus Response— Six and Half a Dozen?

Many people use these two words interchangeably. However, in the context of emotional intelligence, there is a material difference between a reaction and a response. A reaction is comparable to an amygdala hijack in that it is driven by your unconscious mind. It happens without your giving it conscious thought.

In contrast, a response is born out of a conscious decision. It is the result of a thought process during which you weigh the pros and cons of the actions being contemplated. You take into consideration how your actions might impact you as well as other people involved in the situation.

The reality is that, in a given context, a casual observer may not be able to tell the difference between a reaction and a response. That's because the difference between the two lies in the genesis or origin of the action. As stated previously, a reaction emerges from an unconscious process. In contrast, a response is the product of thoughtful consideration of the options available and the application of decision criteria. Examples of decision criteria include your core values and consideration for the impact that your actions might have for you and others beyond the immediate situation.

Therefore, the distinction between a reaction and a response is internal. It may also be temporal. The process of thinking things through and analysing possible outcomes can take time. However, as you develop higher levels of emotional agility, you will find that you navigate the space between stimulus and response much more efficiently. This is consistent with the Conscious Competence[7] Ladder.

---

[7] The Conscious Competence Ladder was conceptualised by Noel Burch of Gordon Training International in the 1970s.

CONSCIOUS COMPETENCY LADDER

Before you started reading this chapter, you were probably on Level 1 of the ladder, in that you were unconsciously unskilled—i.e. generally unaware that you did not possess emotional agility. Having read this far, and hopefully having begun to appreciate what emotional agility is, you are now likely to be at Level 2—consciously unskilled. As you devote time and energy to practice becoming emotionally agile, you will progress to Level 3—consciously skilled. With ongoing diligent practice, ultimately you have the potential to attain Level 4, at which point you become unconsciously skilled at exercising emotional agility. We close this chapter with an exercise designed to help you ascend the Conscious Competence Ladder.

 Self-Reflection Exercise: How Emotionally Agile Are You?

1. Think of a time when you were hijacked by your amygdala. Write down what happened—the circumstances, what happened, how you responded, and the outcome.
2. Describe the emotions that you experienced during the event.

JOAN H. UNDERWOOD

3. What information can you glean from those emotions? What do they communicate to you?

4. Now that you have had some time to think about it, how might you have responded differently—i.e. in a way that is better aligned with your values and intent?

CHAPTER THREE

CULTIVATING WINNING HABITS

*"The chains of habit are too weak to be felt
until they are too strong to be broken."*
–Samuel Johnson

CANNOT RECALL WHEN I FIRST ENCOUNTERED THIS QUOTATION. However, its validity caused it to resonate with me and to become embedded in my mind. The point is aptly illustrated by looking at the habit of smoking cigarettes. Based on my discussions with my grandmother who was a chain smoker for decades, when she took up her first cigarette, there was no intention—or even suspicion—to have it become such an all-consuming activity. However, by the time she realised the power it had over her, it was almost impossible to un-ring the bell.

To successfully transition from high-performing individual contributor to effective manager, there are some habits you need to break and mindsets you need to change. This doesn't necessarily mean they were bad habits or flawed mindsets. It simply means they are no longer fit for purpose. Your purpose has changed from *doing* to *getting things done* with and through others. That means you need to shift gears and focus on actions such as planning, leading, organising, and controlling processes and systems.

That reality is part of the paradox in that you were promoted because of your success as an individual contributor. However, with the promotion, you need to put your glory days as an individual contributor in the file/album of proud accomplishments [NB: It's okay to take them out every now and then to reminisce and reassure yourself that you can accomplish great things] and start figuring out how to master your new role as a manager.

As leaders, we strive to affect behaviour on a daily basis. Veteran managers are all painfully familiar with the disappointment and frustration associated with seeing the changes we have achieved being eroded or completely obliterated when put to the test. That frustration stems from the fact that our aim is to have the change—the new normal—become so ingrained that it is the default response even in the face of challenges and adversity. In other words, we want the desired new behaviour or way of thinking to become habitual.

Six Key Components of a Habit

A working definition of habit is "an acquired behaviour pattern regularly followed until it has become almost involuntary." Julie Dirksen[vi] further breaks down this definition into the following six components:

1. An acquired behaviour pattern—i.e. something learned as opposed to instinctive
2. A trigger which activates the behaviour
3. Motivation on the part of the person displaying the behaviour
4. Feedback—timely, positive reinforcement that helps the behaviour to "stick"

5. Practice—repeating the targeted behaviour until such time that it becomes so ingrained that it can be executed almost subconsciously

6. Environment—conditions or circumstances which support/enable the targeted behaviour.[8]

To illustrate the process, I will share with you my experience in developing the habit of writing on a daily basis (OK, truth be told, it's actually more like five days per week), and ultimately completing the book you're now reading.

1. Acquired Behaviour Pattern: It most definitely wasn't instinctual for me to sit at my computer on a daily basis and write. However, all the published authors I knew—and many I didn't know—insisted that in order to be published, you first have to write.

2. Trigger: For me the trigger was the burning desire to get this book to you. As an HR Manager, then later a Trainer/Facilitator and Executive Coach, I heard about or witnessed the struggle that new supervisors and managers experienced. Even before that, I fought through the struggle myself. My own coaches and mentors and battle scars led me to realise that the journey didn't need to be that painful and traumatic.

3. Motivation: I wanted to make a difference. I wanted to ease the pain, anxiety, and suffering of new managers—to help you get to the point where you become high performers in your new role. However, I must confess that my motives weren't completely altruistic. As a coach, I derive immense pleasure from witnessing the breakthroughs that enable my coachees to take their performance to the next level—to develop and

[8] https://www.td.org/magazines/td-magazine/habitual-by-design

JOAN H. UNDERWOOD

reinforce the self-efficacy that's the hallmark of every successful manager. So my secondary motivation was the psychic income.

4. Feedback: I'm sure you're familiar with the adage that reward sweetens labour. In order for me to continue to work at developing the new habit of daily writing, I needed some form of positive reinforcement or reward. I utilised two mechanisms for this. Firstly, I used a habit tracker—I had a calendar on the wall over my desk, and I placed a check mark on each day when I fulfilled my commitment to write. I also made a promise to myself not to miss two days in a row. The next thing I did was to discipline myself not to have breakfast until I had completed my daily writing assignment. Therefore, sitting down to breakfast became a reward. I confess there were some mornings where hunger was the primary motivator for writing!

5. Practice: While I don't believe that practice makes perfect, I know for certain that it makes progress! But as a recovering perfectionist, I struggled mightily to accept that my daily writing didn't need to be perfect—it just needed to be! Persistence—not perfection—was the goal.

6. Environment: There were two primary conditions or circumstances that helped to reinforce my daily practice of writing—i.e. creating a special or conducive time and place. In terms of time, I decided to link my writing to something to which I was already deeply committed. Due to my family history of heart disease, and my personal history as a survivor of cancer and autoimmune disease, I had previously developed the habit of exercising five days a week. Part of the positive reinforcement for that practice was the surge of endorphins which have been shown to reduce anxiety and boost

self-esteem. What better time to write than when I'm feeling anxiety-free and self-assured? So I made a commitment to do my daily writing immediately after my workout.

7. Having settled on the time, I then needed to identify a place that was conducive to my writing. I'm blessed to live in the Caribbean and doubly blessed to have a home office which is quiet and officially off-limits to anyone other than my husband when I need him to fix something. Therefore, I was guaranteed not to be interrupted during my designated writing time.

 ## Application Exercise: Develop the Essential Habit of Building Relationships

Let's now walk through the process with an example of a new habit that is essential to your success as a manager—building relationships. While we will take a deeper dive into this topic in Part II—Managing Others—this example will help to illustrate how you can succeed in making the practice of building relationships so natural that it becomes almost instinctual. I encourage you to pull out a pen and paper or open your preferred note-taking device and document your responses for each of the six components.

1. What is the targeted behavioural pattern? Establishing and maintaining relationships.
2. What is the trigger to activate the behaviour? If you have already been promoted to a managerial position, that could be considered a trigger. If you have not yet gotten the nod, your desire to secure that appointment could be a sufficient trigger.
3. What is your motivation to establish and maintain relationships? I encourage you to articulate your personal motivation.

JOAN H. UNDERWOOD

However, generally speaking, in order to be an effective manager, you must get things done with and through others. The likelihood of that happening is directly proportional (in fact, the relationship is probably exponential) to the quality of the relationships you have. As we will discuss when we examine persuasion and influence in Chapter 13, people are more likely to cooperate with people they like.

4. What feedback mechanism will you deploy to help the new behaviour to stick? Will a habit tracker work for you as it did for me—i.e. creating a visual to highlight when you fulfilled your commitment—or provide a visual kick in the butt when you didn't? What would constitute an attractive and viable way for you to reward yourself? Conversely, what will be the negative reinforcement for those occasions when you fall off the wagon?

5. What practice regimen will you establish—as in, how often will you commit to working on building or maintaining relationships? Huge word of caution here—it can be tempting to go for a big, audacious goal. Resist that temptation with all your might! This is definitely a case where smaller is better. When building a new habit, it is important to make the practice as simple and as easy as possible. Remember that daily writing habit I developed? I started out with seven minutes. That's it! In making that determination, I was guided by the advice of Dr. BJ Fogg in his book *Tiny Habits* where he stated that the goal was not volume, but rather making the habit easy to achieve.

6. Clearly I didn't write this entire book in seven-minute instalments. However, in the beginning, that was the extent of the commitment I made. The fact that it was manageable made it easier for me to establish the habit. So in practical terms, what

does that mean for you and your new habit of establishing and maintaining relationships? Perhaps your targeted habit will be to engage one person each day (or week) in a 2 to 3-minute conversation about a topic unrelated to work... Remember, make it manageable—and write it down!

7. What conditions or circumstances will you put in place to support you in carrying out the targeted behaviour? In my example of establishing a daily writing habit, I told you how I utilised time and place. What will work best for you? What is something that you currently do (as in, an existing habit) and to which you can attach this new habit? For example, do you take a daily coffee break in the lunchroom? Do a weekly walk-through of the department? Pass by several cubicles on your way back from the washroom? Could you "stick on" or attach a 2 to 3-minute non-work related conversation to a direct report, peer, or boss to those or other existing habits?

Another valuable tool to help build new habits is accountability. The Association for Talent Development (ATD) conducted a study which found that the chances of completing a goal are 65% if you share that commitment with someone. The likelihood of success rockets to 95% if you have a specific accountability appointment with someone. Therefore, if you decide that you will have X number of 2 to 3-minute non-work-related conversations this month and set up an appointment with Person Y to provide an update on your success rate, there's a 95% probability that you will hit your target. Why not give it a try to see if ATD and I got it right?

So you now have a plan to cultivate a winning habit that is essential to your success as a manager. As you read over what you've prepared in this exercise, it might seem insignificant. I hope it does, because then you're less likely to make up excuses for not doing it.

JOAN H. UNDERWOOD

In the words of James Clear,[vii] author of *Atomic Habits*, changes that seem small and unimportant at first will compound into remarkable results if you're willing to stick with them for years.[9]

---

[9] https://jamesclear.com/atomic-habits

CHAPTER FOUR

BECOMING CHANGE ABLE

*"Embrace change. True success can be defined by
your ability to adapt to changing circumstances."*

–Ritu Ghatourey

I N THE PREVIOUS CHAPTER, I MENTIONED THAT YOU WOULD NEED to change some of your existing habits and mindsets. I also acknowledged that that was easier said than done. In this chapter, I provide some guidelines on how to become more Change Able—i.e. willing and able to anticipate and adapt to changing circumstances.

Holocaust survivor and bestselling author Viktor Frankl[10] pointed out that when we are no longer able to change a situation, it's time to change ourselves. Based on his writings, Frankl was persuaded that it was that change ability that enabled him and thousands of others to survive the Holocaust. While your situation is nowhere near as dire as what confronted Frankl and other Jews during the Holocaust, the reality is that you cannot change the fact that change is inevitable. What you *can* change is your attitude towards change and how you respond to it.

---

[10] Frankl was an Austrian psychologist and author of *Man's Search for Meaning.*

Based on your level within the organisation, you will have to navigate changes which are mandated from the organisational hierarchy (higher-ups), as well as those you initiate yourself as part of your quest to improve your team's effectiveness and efficiency. By becoming change able, you can master both types of changes.

Kubler-Ross Change Curve

While it has been criticised for being overly simplistic, I personally find Elizabeth Kubler-Ross's [viii] Change Curve to be a useful way of conceptualizing the range of emotions that are typically associated with the human response to change.

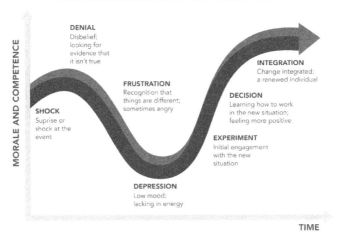

THE KUBLER-ROSS CHANGE CURVE

Kubler-Ross's model describes a range of emotions we tend to experience in response to change. While the emotions in question are typically mapped against time, it is important to note that the progression from one emotion to another is not linear, and that individuals may not necessarily experience all the emotions shown on the curve.

Let us examine each of the emotions on the curve and their outward manifestations.

Shock: Upon receiving news of the change, you may be shocked or surprised—especially if you were not aware of the circumstances driving the need for the change.

Denial: Shock may give way to denial or disbelief. During this stage of the change curve, you may actively seek out evidence that it's all a big mistake—that all the talk about change is just a rumour and that nothing will really come of it.

Frustration: As time goes on, and it becomes evident that the change is really happening, you may experience frustration or even anger. This is especially likely if you thought things were okay as they were.

Depression: The realization that the change is happening may also lead to depression or at least concern about how the change is likely to impact you.

Experiment: Once you realise that this is happening, you may get curious and decide to get more information—to check things out.

Decision: Based on the information gleaned during your experimentation phase, you may decide that the change isn't that bad after all. In fact, you may come to the realization that it's actually an improvement over what previously existed.

Integration: During this stage of the process, the change becomes your new normal. You integrate it into your way of doing things, and it becomes the status quo—at least until the next change...

JOAN H. UNDERWOOD

Your Attitude Towards Change

Several factors determine how quickly you move through the change curve and whether you experience all the elements in the curve. Some of those factors—such as your employer's approach to change management—are not necessarily within your control. The variable over which you have complete control is your *attitude* towards change.

If you choose to see yourself as a victim of change, then you are likely to get stuck in the first half of the curve—in shock, disbelief, frustration, and depression. Those are all emotions which drain your energy. And when your energy is drained, it becomes even more difficult to manage effectively.

On the other hand, if you choose (remember emotional agility) to be change able, you approach the situation with an open mindset. This paves the way for you to experiment with the change with a view to identifying how you can best integrate it into your routine.

The most effective attitude that you can adopt towards change is one of resilience. Once you choose to adopt a resilient mindset, you convince yourself that you can and will move forward (I reject the notion of bouncing back, since change is intended to have forward momentum), and that any challenges and adversity associated with the change are actually opportunities for personal and/or professional growth and development.

Your Ability to Change

Once you have a change able mindset, you then need to match it with some action. The secret sauce here is agility—the ability to be comfortable with being uncomfortable during the change process. Agility is what enables you to experiment with the change until you get to the point where you figure out what works best and then proceed to integrate it into your new normal.

This type of agility is not automatic. It's a competence that you need to build. One of my favourite tools to help accomplish this task is the ADKAR Model.[11] As a Prosci® Certified Change Practitioner, I've found that—in addition to being an effective tool for organisational change management—ADKAR has great utility in equipping individuals to survive and thrive during organisational change. Let's look at each of the elements in the model and examine how they can help you to become change able.

Awareness: This refers to the awareness of the need for change—i.e. the *why* of it. As someone who has decided to take responsibility for your success as a manager, if the why is not presented to you by your organisation, I encourage you to seek it out. The specific questions to which you should seek answers include:

1. What is the precise nature of the upcoming change?
2. What is driving this change? Why is it necessary or advisable?
3. What is the risk (both to the organisation and to me personally) of not changing?

In a best-case scenario, your employer will provide this information as part of the organisation's change management process. However, let's not kid ourselves. Research has shown that 70% of change initiatives fail, and the primary reason they do is because organisations don't pay enough attention to the people side of change. Therefore, in all likelihood, it's probably going to be up to you to seek out this information.

---

[11] The ADKAR Model of Change was developed by Prosci based on their research conducted over fourteen years and involving more than 2,600 companies. For more information, visit https://www.prosci.com/adkar/adkar-model

JOAN H. UNDERWOOD

Desire: Once you become aware of the factors driving the change, the next required element is to develop the desire to be part of the process. This corresponds to the decision component of Kubler-Ross's change curve. To cultivate desire, here is a series of questions you should ask yourself:

1. What's in this for me (WIIFM)?
2. Am I prepared to make a personal choice to support this change?
3. If I am not prepared to support this change, am I prepared to accept the consequences of not doing so?

It's important to be brutally honest with yourself in assessing your level of desire to contribute to the successful implementation of the change. Given your role as a manager, you need to either commit to the change *or* get out of the way *or* risk being rolled over by the big change machine as it makes its way down the road.

Knowledge: Once you've decided that you will be supporting the change, your next area of focus should be on ensuring you have the knowledge required to make a meaningful contribution. The relevant questions at this stage include:

1. Do I understand exactly what the change means for me and how I operate within the organisation?
2. What training do I need for the new process/tools?

Ability: While having knowledge is a necessary condition, it is not sufficient. You also need the ability to execute. Maybe this confession will help you to remember the distinction between knowledge and ability. I know what is required to ride a bicycle. I can even describe the mechanics of it to you. However, I'm ashamed to say that—due to a very traumatic incident involving me, my neighbour's bicycle, and a very hard concrete road—I lack the *ability* to ride a bicycle. Therefore, my knowledge is of little use to me—or anyone else for that matter!

To help ensure that you have the ability to change, here are a few questions you need to ask and answer.

1. What skills do I need to acquire to successfully implement this change?
2. What behaviours do I need to adopt to effect this change?

Reinforcement: You will recall that the final element in Kubler-Ross's change curve is integration. Reinforcement is your way of ensuring the change remains integrated—that you do not revert to the old way of doing things. An organisation skilled at change management will put systems in place to reinforce the change. Such systems can be in the form of positive reinforcement to reward those who implement the change. Alternatively, steps may be taken to discourage or punish those who do not comply.

In addition to whatever mechanisms the organisation puts in place, as a change able manager who has the ability to self-regulate, you should also institute your personal reinforcement system to help ensure that you stay the course—at least, until it's time for the next cycle of changes. After all, I'm sure you already know that the only thing that's constant is change.

 **Application Exercise: Develop your Ability to Manage Change**

Think of a change that's happening in your life. It can be either personal or professional. With that specific change in mind, please answer the following questions.

1. **Awareness:** What is driving this change? Why is it happening? If the change doesn't happen, what are the likely consequences or outcomes?
2. **Desire:** How might this change benefit you? How prepared are you to support the change? If you decide not to support the change, are you prepared to accept the consequences of that decision?
3. **Knowledge:** What exactly does the change mean for you and how you do things? What do you need to know/learn to successfully navigate the change?
4. **Ability:** What new skills, behaviours, or other resources do you need to implement the change?
5. **Reinforcement:** What can you put in place to help you stick with the change once implementation begins?

CHAPTER FIVE

WHERE THE BUCK STOPS

Poor leaders ask, "Who's at fault?"
Strong leaders ask, "Where did the process break down?"
—Michael Timms

I N JULY 2016, AN ACCUSED MURDERER ESCAPED FROM A COURT-house in Broward County, Florida. In the immediate aftermath, the Broward County sheriff blamed the county commission for the prisoner's escape. In fact, his statement to the press began and ended with him blasting the county for failing to provide adequate funding to his department. Somewhere in between his castigation of the commission, he mentioned that the prisoner was armed and extremely dangerous...

The commission was quick to respond, detailing how much money they had allocated and questioning whether the sheriff had effectively and efficiently utilised the money for the designated purpose. Based on those facts as reported, both the sheriff and the commission were operating on the lower rungs of the accountability ladder in that they were exclusively focused on assigning blame and making excuses. Neither party accepted responsibility. The statements of both parties reflected a mindset of powerlessness.

ACCOUNTABILITY LADDER

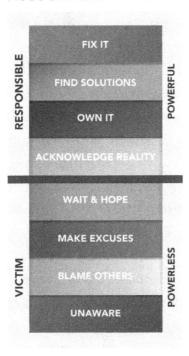

I encourage you right here and now, as a new manager, to resolve to operate from the upper rungs of the Accountability Ladder—to strive for personal responsibility and power. But just before you make that commitment, let's ensure you understand and appreciate the difference between blame, responsibility, and accountability.

Blame

Blame focuses exclusively on finding fault. As such, it anchors itself in the past with no orientation towards the future. It has a distinctively punitive orientation—as opposed to a desire to learn and improve.

If you allow the focus to remain on blame, there is no guarantee the undesired outcome will not be repeated; there is no guarantee you will learn from the experience.

So, if we return to the matter of the Broward County sheriff's budget, let's suppose for a moment that the sheriff succeeded in pinning the blame on the county commission. Let's further assume that, having been so named and shamed, the commission decided to open the coffers and invite the sheriff to take as much money as he would like. What would be best use of said funds? It's impossible to say, since neither the sheriff nor the commission took the time to thoroughly investigate what transpired. As a result, they were unable to diagnose all the vulnerabilities in the system or identify the role played by human error or other contributing factors. Therefore, even if they spent all the money in the county's budget, there could be no guarantee that the security problems would be rectified.

Another predictable consequence of playing the blame game is the deterioration of working relationships. Imagine for a moment how you would feel if your manager threw you under the bus when a project went sideways—i.e. didn't pan out as anticipated. How inclined would you be to go the extra mile for that manager in the future?

Responsibility

In the context of our current discussion, the word "responsible" is value neutral—i.e. it's not inherently good or bad. A working definition for *responsibility* is having an obligation to do something, or having control over or care for someone, as part of one's job or role. The Broward County sheriff, by virtue of the authority vested in his position, was responsible for the care and control of the prisoners in the courthouse that day.

People in whom responsibility is vested are expected to be reliable and effective in executing their assigned roles and associated responsibilities. Therefore, there is usually an expectation that they will be answerable for their performance. And that brings us to your new role as manager.

Your new job description outlines your duties and areas of responsibility. Your employer has a reasonable expectation that you will execute your new role with due care and diligence. What exactly does that mean? As a new manager, you are expected to acknowledge the realities that exist within the department/unit you manage; that you will own what happens within your chain of command; that you will find solutions to the problems that exist; and that you will proceed to implement the best possible solutions in order to fix said problems. In other words, your employer expects you to be accountable.

Accountability

Our working definition for accountability is the condition wherein a person is expected to take ownership of their actions or decisions. Accountability follows from responsibility in that you are called to give account for your handling of the area of responsibility.

While, as previously stated, responsibility is value-neutral, accountability tends to come into play when the outcome of the administration of your responsibility is less than, or otherwise inconsistent with, expectations or agreed performance standards.

In the case of the escape from the courthouse, in pursuit of accountability, the sheriff should have investigated—or caused to be investigated—the sequence of events to identify exactly how the prisoner was able to escape, where exactly security was breached/compromised, and what measures could be put in place to rectify any weaknesses in the system.

While accountability is based on past performance, it is

future-oriented. By this I mean that it is geared towards extracting lessons from what has transpired to influence future performance and secure better outcomes. This contrasts sharply with blame.

Proof of Concept on the Battlefield

Several years ago, while serving as the Regional Project Manager (RPM) for a twenty-million-dollar project covering twelve Caribbean countries, I found myself in the middle of a potentially catastrophic snafu. I'll share my battle scars with you if you promise to utilise it as a cautionary tale.

The flagship programme in that project was an itinerant, multi-module leadership development programme. That meant that every six weeks or so, the programme training cohort travelled to one of the twelve participating countries to attend a five-day, face-to-face learning module. This particular module took place in St. Kitts. That is significant in that the co-chairman of the project's Steering Committee (a.k.a. my boss) resided in St. Kitts. In addition to being my boss, Sir K. Dwight Venner was the governor of the Eastern Caribbean Central Bank, and the man who conceptualised the project and almost single-handedly persuaded the Canadian Government to fund it. Bottom line is, he was a big deal as far as this project was concerned.

It had become the norm to launch each module of the programme with an opening ceremony featuring speeches by the Head of Government from the host country, representatives of the Canadian Government, and members of the cohort of regional leaders. All speeches tended to acknowledge the role of Sir K. Dwight Venner in conceptualising the project and serving as co-chair of the Steering Committee. So, of course, being in the country where he resided, he was scheduled to deliver the feature address at this particular opening ceremony.

The time drew near for the ceremony to commence. In my role as

JOAN H. UNDERWOOD

the RPM, I also served as the master of ceremonies. I was a bit concerned that the governor was late. So I called his office to inquire about his estimated time of arrival. I was absolutely flabbergasted when his executive assistant indicated that there was nothing booked in the governor's calendar for that morning. After all, this event had been in the planning stages for several months. How on earth could it not be in his calendar?

Decision point: I have a room of dignitaries and invited guests—including the media—waiting for the commencement of this high-profile opening ceremony. I'm missing my keynote speaker. So what should I do?

In that moment, I had to decide whether to cling to the bottom rungs of the accountability ladder. The actions likely to flow from that choice included:

- Announcing that I had no idea what had gone wrong
- Blaming my staff for failing to ensure that the necessary invitation was issued to the governor
- Making excuses for what was obviously a lapse on our part
- Waiting and hoping that the governor would rearrange his calendar and put in a late appearance

That entire menu of options would have positioned me as a powerless victim in the face of a potential crisis.

The other decision pathway—i.e. the top rungs of the accountability ladder—included the following actions:

- Acknowledging the unfortunate reality
- Owning it—taking responsibility for what had transpired and the associated adverse outcomes for the various stakeholders
- Identifying and implementing solutions
- Putting the necessary measures in place to make sure it didn't happen again

So, I inhaled deeply and jumped onto the top rungs of the ladder... I placed a call to my staff member who was responsible for liaising with the governor's office and issued a simple and unambiguous request—that she prepare and submit before close of business a report detailing the following:

- What went wrong?
- Why did it happen?
- What measures should be put in place to eliminate the possibility of a repeat of this situation?

My approach to this matter was predicated on my personal leadership philosophy and the type of culture that I had established within the organisation. As a leader, I had chosen to create a culture of accountability rather than one of blame. I've highlighted some of the practical differences in the table below.[12]

Characteristics	Culture of Blame	Culture of Accountability
Believes...	People are the problem	People are problem solvers
	Problems are headaches	Problems are learning opportunities
	Admitting weaknesses is career limiting	We are all still learning
Focuses on...	Who is wrong	What is wrong
	Fault-finding	Fact-finding
	Assigning punishment	Improving future results
Results in...	Hiding problems	Surfacing problems and solutions
	Naming and shaming	Learning from mistakes
	Distrust	Trust

---

[12] This content is informed by the work of Michael Timms of Avail Leadership.

JOAN H. UNDERWOOD

Adhering to a culture of accountability paid significant dividends in that the requested report was not all that I received. I also earned the loyalty and respect of the staff member in question. From that point forward, she knew without a doubt that I had her back and that, as her manager, I would hold her accountable for her actions—as well as her errors of omission—but I would never throw her under the bus.

We all have responsibilities. Inevitably things will go wrong at some point in time—either in spite of us or because of us. When that happens, we have a choice of pursuing blame or accountability.

If you choose the blame option, your mission is accomplished as soon as you have identified someone at whom you can point an accusatory finger and punish them for what happened. In that situation, the primary outcomes are most likely to be damaged relationships/reputations and a missed opportunity for personal and organisational growth and development.

However, if you choose the accountability path, you adopt a mindset characterised by curiosity and the sincere desire to learn and improve. You extract lessons and carry them forward to secure better outcomes in the future.

As a new manager, which culture will you choose to create within your team?

CHAPTER SIX

AN ATTITUDE OF GRATITUDE

"When we focus on our gratitude, the tide of disappointment goes out and the tide of love rushes in."

–Kristin Armstrong[ix]

LEADING UP TO THE 2016 PRESIDENTIAL ELECTIONS IN THE USA, the majority of media outlets and their lineup of pundits predicted a victory for Hillary Clinton. So, when Donald Trump pulled off the victory that caught most of the world off guard, my attention turned to how Hillary Clinton would react in the face of the stunning defeat. As I listened to her concession speech, I was struck by a number of things—chief among them was the fact that she used the words "gratitude" or "thank you" sixteen times in a twelve-minute speech.

Upon reflecting on that, my mind went to the value of choosing to adopt an attitude of gratitude. I imagine that the realization she had lost the elections elicited many emotions in Mrs. Clinton. Of course, I can't know for sure what motivated her decision to adopt and display an attitude of gratitude. What I do know is that neuroscience has shown that expressing gratitude provides significant benefits in both the immediate and long term.

Oprah's Life Class

Oprah is on record as saying that starting and maintaining a gratitude journal has been the single most powerful decision she ever made—that from a woman who has accomplished so much, a woman who has made decisions that have multi-million-dollar consequences…

The cynic in me looks at our lead quotation and says, "Yeah, but remember that the tide goes out only to come back in again!" Here's the thing, though—when we choose to express gratitude consistently and repeatedly, something profound happens. Just ask Oprah…

> *"If you pull the lever of gratitude every day,*
> *you'll be amazed at the results."*
> *—Oprah*

The Neuroscience of Gratitude

So, what is really behind this gratitude hype? Is it just another touchy-feely fad that will pass? Actually, there's real science behind it. Neuroscience has confirmed what Oprah and so many others have discovered—that expressing gratitude really does make you feel good. Why? It turns out that expressing gratitude produces the same outcome as one gets from using antidepressants. Specifically, expressing gratitude increases our levels of dopamine and serotonin, thereby creating feelings of contentment.

Further to that, the more often we choose to express gratitude, the more natural it becomes. Here again, there is a scientific underpinning to this assertion—i.e. Hebb's Law. In essence, Hebb's Law states that neurons that fire together, wire together. Expressed differently, the more times a certain neural pathway is activated (neurons firing together), the less effort it takes to stimulate the pathway the next time (neurons wiring together).

By regularly expressing gratitude—e.g. through a journal, as recommended by Oprah—we create a habit system that redounds to our benefit.

Here's the thing, though—if you opt instead to focus on the negatives, that, too, can become a habit. Unfortunately, it has none of the positive mental and physical health benefits associated with the habit of expressing gratitude.

Zulie Rain endorsed that point in her May 2020 blog post captioned "Six Habits of Deeply Miserable People."[13] The lack of gratitude had the dubious distinction of clocking in at habit #6. Rain described the lack of gratitude as the most persistent trait of deeply miserable people. She went on to suggest that such people are so fixated on what could go wrong, they are unable to acknowledge and appreciate the good things—no matter how small or large they are.

Another blogger, Paula Lawes,[x] was able to come up with fifteen habits of highly miserable people. Guess what topped her list? Lawes opined that miserable people avoid expressing gratitude at all costs since doing so goes against their belief system. A girlfriend of mine perhaps expresses the paradox best when she says that some people just aren't "happy" unless they find something to be miserable about!

Practical Benefits of Gratitude

So, while I can't promise you that the daily expression of gratitude will bring you Oprah-like financial success, according to researchers at Eastern Washington University, there is significant positive

[13] https://medium.com/mind-cafe/six-habits-of-deeply-miserable-people-1e60f8ad123e

JOAN H. UNDERWOOD

correlation between the habitual expression of gratitude and the following positive effects:

- Feeling a sense of abundance in one's life
- Appreciating the contributions of others to one's wellbeing
- Recognizing and enjoying life's small pleasures
- Acknowledging the importance of experiencing and expressing gratitude

If that doesn't do it for you, how about the fact that people who regularly express gratitude experience more positive emotions, feel more alive, sleep better, show more compassion and kindness, and even have stronger immune systems?

Application Exercise:
Start a Gratitude Journal

At this point, I hope you're persuaded that expressing gratitude is a good thing and that it's good for you. As you step into your role as manager, the statistics are stacked against you. You already have something positive going for you—you're reading this book. As a result, you are aware of the pitfalls, and you're in the process of learning how to overcome them. However, the fact remains that 60% of new managers fail or underperform in their first two years.[14]

A lot of things can go wrong. You have a choice—you can join the camp of deeply miserable people as described by Rain and Lawes, or you can choose to adopt an attitude of gratitude. My hope is that you go with the latter option. In the off chance you decide to do so, here are some steps to help you along the way.

---

[14] Research conducted by CEB Global—now Gartner.

1. Get a book/journal to use for this exercise. If you—like me—aren't big on writing by hand, start a file on the device of your choice.

2. At the end of each day, call to mind at least one thing that happened for which you are grateful. It doesn't matter how small or how big it is. No matter how crappy a day you had, find at least one thing or one person for whom you can be grateful. (NB: Don't be miserable! You can do this!)

3. Make a record in your journal—be specific. Your sentence should start "I am grateful that…" or "I am grateful for…"

4. Then record the feeling(s)/emotion(s) you experienced as a result of that event or having that person in your life at that particular moment in time.

5. Sit quietly for a few moments and savour the benefits of being grateful.

CHAPTER SEVEN

YOU CAN'T POUR FROM AN EMPTY CUP

"Just when you feel you have no time to relax, know that this is the moment you most need to make time to relax."
—Matt Haig[xi]

"Self-care is never a selfish act—it is simply good stewardship of the only gift I have, the gift I was put on earth to offer others. Anytime we can listen to true self and give the care it requires, we do it not only for ourselves, but for the many others whose lives we touch."
—Parker Palmer[xii]

IN THE QUEST FOR SUCCESS, YOU JUST MIGHT FIND YOURSELF BURNING the candle at both ends. In fact, research has shown that some leaders wear self-sacrifice—including sleep deprivation—as a badge of honour. While the intention behind this mindset may be noble, the practice is both unsustainable and self-defeating.

During the first quarter of 2020—just before the onset of the COVID-19 Pandemic—I conducted a survey of Caribbean professionals. My aim was to investigate the level of stress and the various coping strategies utilised to help overcome stress. The results were worrisome but not surprising.

In response to a question about the number of hours spent at work on a weekly basis, 51% of survey respondents indicated that they averaged forty to fifty hours per week. The corresponding percentage for fifty to sixty hours was 31%. Therefore, 82% of the population sample indicated that they worked between forty and sixty hours per week.

Respondents also provided information about their sleeping habits. Sixty-one percent of respondents indicated that they averaged less than six hours of sleep nightly. The majority (i.e. 58%) said that they averaged between four and six hours per night. To place this in context, the Mayo Clinic maintains that adults should get between seven and nine hours of sleep nightly.

Survey respondents were also asked to place themselves on a spectrum which ranged from feeling comfortable to feeling stressed. The midrange of the spectrum was described as stretched. Forty-two percent of respondents self-identified as being stressed; 37% indicated they were stretched; and 21% said they were comfortable.

So, the bottom line is that the majority of this sample of Caribbean professionals is working extra-long hours, suffering from sleep deprivation, and feeling stretched to stressed. Yet they soldier on... They are, in essence, continuing to pour from depleted cups. As you navigate your new role as a manager, it is absolutely essential—for your personal wellbeing as well as in the interest of professional success—that you develop and maintain the habit of replenishing your cup.

Survey respondents were also asked to identify the measures they used to relieve stress. The most common responses were exercise

JOAN H. UNDERWOOD

(58%), music (57%), spending time with loved ones (52%), and prayer or religion (49%). The next most popular coping strategies were meditation, reading, eating, and consuming alcohol or pharmaceuticals.

Over the years, there are ten stress-busters which have worked wonders for me personally as well as for my coaching clients. I share them with you along with encouragement to incorporate them into your daily or weekly routine. In other words, don't wait until you're feeling overwhelmed to engage in these activities. Don't wait until your cup is empty to take action. Rather, make it a habit to replenish your cup at regular intervals.

Ten Practices to Replenish Your Cup

1. Exercise/Move: In addition to the obvious health benefits, exercise contributes to our emotional wellbeing. The hormones released during exercise reduce anxiety and boost self-esteem.
2. Sleep: Ensure you work towards getting at least seven hours' sleep nightly. Research has shown that anything less than that is likely to have a detrimental effect on how you function throughout the day.
3. Proper Nutrition: Food is the body's fuel. If we consume low-grade fuel, we can't expect to have a high-performance body or mind.
4. Practice Mindfulness: Be fully present in each moment. Resist the temptation to spend your now worrying about what might happen tomorrow or what went wrong yesterday.
5. Express Gratitude: Scientific research has shown that expressing gratitude can lower blood pressure, improve immune function, and facilitate more efficient sleep. Besides, Oprah said it's good for you!

6. Make/Create Something: The creative process results in a sense of accomplishment, which can be quite self-affirming and validating. So, whether your preferred medium is arts and craft, cooking, gardening, or a DIY project, set aside the stress of work and get your hands dirty.

7. Engage in Positive Imagery: Neuroscience has confirmed that the brain doesn't distinguish between an imagined experience and an actual experience. So, when you visualise your happy place, your brain has the same neurochemical response as if you were actually there.

Years ago, I was coaching a senior executive who became extremely anxious whenever he had to make a presentation to the board of directors. In working through the issue, we conducted a visualisation exercise which took him back to a memory of when he had been extremely successful. The memory he selected was a cricket match from his school days. He had scored the winning run in a match between his school and their archrival. During the visualisation exercise, he relived every detail of the experience—not just seeing it, but feeling what was happening on the outside (e.g. weather conditions, spectators in the stands, placement of his teammates on the field), as well as the emotions he experienced. As we went through the exercise, his posture changed; his tone of voice changed; his facial expressions changed. He once again became powerful, victorious, elated… By reliving that victory before he stepped into the boardroom, he summoned those same emotions and leveraged them to achieve a confident, powerful interaction with his board.

8. Connect with Others: Humans are social beings. We are not meant to live in isolation. That's why solitary confinement is considered punishment. So make the time to connect with

others. The connection to which I'm referring here is human to human. Your focus shouldn't be on a task but rather on bonding with another human being.

9. Ask for/Accept Support: One of the biggest myths causing us unnecessary stress is that it's a sign of weakness to ask for or accept help. That's the devil talking. Rebuke that liar!

10. BREATHE: Take a few deep, cleansing, calming breaths and reassure yourself. This too shall pass.

Pitfalls of Perfectionism

There was a time in my life where I actually thought it was a compliment when people described me as a perfectionist. I thought they were paying homage to my high standards. Over time, I came to realise that being a perfectionist was doing me more harm than good—that I was missing out on opportunities simply because I wasn't willing to try new things unless I was absolutely certain I would excel at them. Perhaps even more importantly, I realised I was causing my staff undue stress.

You know what's not a synonym for perfectionism? Flexibility! While flexibility and perfectionism don't exactly hang out in the same circles, flexibility is the close companion of psychological health and wellbeing.

My perfectionism had a benign/well-intentioned origin. My quest for excellence was ingrained in me largely due to my Catholic school upbringing. From the age of four to the age of fifteen, I recited and pledged to adhere to the school motto—Excelsior! Higher Yet!

Don't get me wrong, the motto served me well in many instances. However, the lack of flexibility that I internalised along with the motto led to suboptimal behaviours, like continuing habits beyond their usefulness, over-delivering when I didn't have to—and when it didn't actually add meaningful value—and to overthinking almost every decision I made.

During my days as an unreformed perfectionist, it didn't occur to me that there was such a thing as an unimportant decision. Therefore, I habitually and automatically classified everything as being worthy of my full effort. I treated the simplest work task as if it were an Olympic sport with a gold medal as the only acceptable outcome.

Since my perfectionist affliction went into remission, I regularly review the opportunity cost of any activity or behaviour in order to make sure that it represents the best use of my physical and mental energy *or* that I'll have fun doing it.

You know something else that doesn't travel in the same circles as perfectionism? Tolerance. Take it from this reformed perfectionist, to succeed in your new role as a manager, if tolerance isn't already in your toolkit, you're going to need to start acquiring it in wholesale quantities.

Tolerance is a gift to yourself as well as to the people you lead. So, while you're replenishing your cup, go ahead and pour yourself a generous portion.

PART II
MANAGING OTHERS

CHAPTER EIGHT

BUILDING TRUST

"As a boss, you can demand compliance but you must earn commitment, and the coin of that realm is trust."

–Linda Hill & Kent Lineback

L EADERSHIP IS ABOUT GETTING THINGS DONE WITH AND THROUGH others. The command-and-control approach to leadership won't get you very far—unless you're in a military or paramilitary organisation (or a cult). The rest of us get things done through influence and persuasion, which we will explore in depth in Chapter 13. For now, suffice it to say that trust is an essential building block if you are to succeed in your new role as a manager.

It's important to note that trust doesn't just benefit you as an individual manager. Rather, the benefits accrue to the entire organisation and manifest as a Trust Dividend.

According to research conducted by Paul J Zak,[xiii] compared with people at low-trust companies, people at high-trust companies report: 74% less stress, 106% more energy at work, 50% higher productivity, 13% fewer sick days, 76% more engagement, 29% more satisfaction with their lives, and 40% less burnout. So how can you accumulate this trust dividend or coin of the realm? The solution lies in what some may consider counterintuitive—i.e. to gain trust, you must be trustworthy yourself. In other words, you must apply the law of the harvest and sow the seed if you want to reap the fruit.

Four Components of Trust

There is a tendency to view trust as an all-or-nothing variable—either you trust someone or you don't. In reality, it's much more nuanced and contextual than that. It is useful to break down the concept of trust into four elements—namely competence, character, benevolence, and consistency. When you don't trust someone, that could be because…

- You question their competence or ability to complete the task at hand; or
- You may have doubts/questions about their character—i.e. their honesty or integrity; or
- You have reason to question whether they have your best interests at heart; or
- Their past performance has been inconsistent, thereby creating some doubt/concern about whether they will deliver this time around.

Let's take a deeper dive into each of the four components of trust.

COMPONENTS OF TRUST

CONSISTENCY

BENEVOLENCE

CHARACTER

COMPETENCE

© Copyright UTDS INC. 2020

Competence

Competency-based trust stems from the belief that someone possesses the requisite knowledge, skills, and abilities to execute the assigned functions. You may have noticed that I didn't mention qualifications. In some cases, qualifications are a prerequisite for even being considered to fill a given role. However, while qualifications may help you to land that dream job, to inspire trust and hold on to it, you must be able to deliver the goods.

Character

"The measure of a man's character is what he would do if he knew he never would be found out." Thomas Macaulay reached that conclusion in the mid-nineteenth century. It is just as valid today as it was then.

For the purpose of this discussion, character can be defined as the collection of attributes that determines a person's moral and ethical actions and reactions. Since these attributes themselves are not visible or tangible, the people with whom you interact will rely on your behaviour to deduce the content of your character. Therefore, it is important to bear in mind that, in your new role as manager, you are casting a long shadow. Direct reports, peers, and bosses will be observing your actions and using those observations to draw conclusions about your character and, by extension, your trustworthiness. I invite you to choose today what attributes you want to be reflected in your character.

Benevolence

Shortly after I graduated from university, an older and wiser person advised me that people don't care how much you know until they know how much you care. Over the years, I would have occasion to remember those sage words. If you want to earn people's trust—whether those people are your direct reports, peers, managers, or customers—the first thing you have to do is to prove to them you truly care, that you wish them well. That is the essence of benevolence.

Consistency

There's a reason why I've opted to present this as the final component. Consistency refers to the extent to which you can be relied upon to always perform in a similar way or to a comparable standard. I invite you to view consistency as a meta-component of trust. Your level of trustworthiness is dependent on the extent to which you are consistent in manifesting the three other components—competence, character, and benevolence. For example, can you think of a co-worker who is technically proficient but who is completely unreliable? Do you trust that person to deliver for you or for the team every time you need them to? Or what about that person you just can't figure out, because they seem to blow hot and cold—one moment they act like you're their best friend, and on another occasion, they don't seem inclined to give you the time of day. How much would you *trust* such a person?

Overcoming a Trust Deficit

As you consider the four elements of trust we've just examined, I invite you to turn the mirror on yourself. How trustworthy are you in your role as a new/aspiring supervisor/manager? As stated in Chapter 1, self-awareness is a precursor to wisdom and to self-regulation. Is this a blind spot for you?

If a trust deficit exists, how can you go about rectifying that situation? Since trust is nuanced and contextual, it follows logically that the strategies for resolving a trust deficit are also contextual. Generally speaking, the easiest deficit to rectify is one related to competency. If there is a gap in your knowledge, skills, or abilities, and you are sufficiently motivated, you can take steps to acquire the necessary knowledge, skills, and abilities.

Based on my experiences as an HR practitioner over the last two decades, I strongly encourage you to take ownership of your professional development. Far too often, people self-sabotage by abdicating this responsibility and depending on the employer (or a manager, mentor, or sponsor) to take the lead in identifying and procuring training and development opportunities for them. I challenge you to become your own best advocate. Be proactive in identifying current and potential competency gaps and how you can go about closing them. You can accomplish this either under your own steam or with financial or in-kind support from your employer.

If there is something that has caused members of your team to question your character, it will take more than talk to eliminate that trust deficit. The most effective remediation comes from consistently authentic actions and the passage of time. This can be a particularly bitter pill to swallow if you think the individual has misinterpreted you, your actions, and/or your motives. However, it's important to remember that perception is reality. So, quite frankly, whether or not you think their concerns are legitimate is irrelevant. Therefore, my advice to you is to focus on your actions going forward, ensuring that they are transparent and that they genuinely reflect your core values.

Research has shown that the level of employee engagement is directly related to the quality of the relationship with one's direct supervisor or manager. A primary determinant of that quality is the individual's perception of the level of authenticity of your interest and concern. In order for you to leverage discretionary effort from the members of your team, they must believe that you mean them well—that you're not seeking to manipulate them or take advantage of them in some other way.

A benevolence-related trust deficit is arguably the most difficult to rectify. If members of your team suspect you don't mean them well, you're already off-balance on a downward, slippery slope. The bottom line is that it's hard to recover from a benevolence-related trust deficit, and it's not likely to end well. Therefore, I recommend you do everything within your power to ensure your words and deeds send an unequivocal message that you genuinely care about your team members—both individually and collectively. This means putting in the groundwork starting from day one and continuing each day thereafter.

And that brings us back to our meta-component—i.e. consistency. In order to build and maintain trust in your relationships with your direct reports, peers, bosses, and customers, you need to show up in a way that convinces them that, as sure as the sun rises in the east and sets in the west, they can bank on the fact your actions will be those of someone who is competent, of good character, and who has their best interests at heart.

Caveat

One final word on trust before we move on to explore the other essential building blocks of effective relationships—having trusting relationships does not mean that things will never go wrong, or that storm clouds will never darken your horizon. Rather, what it means is that when the bad weather comes along—as it inevitably will—the relationship will have the structural integrity to withstand the external pressures brought on by the storm.

Another useful metaphor is that of maintaining a bank account. If you develop the habit of making regular deposits into that account, the balance will grow to the point that when the need arises to cover a major expense, you would have accumulated enough funds to cover it without going into overdraft. So it is with trust—work diligently and consistently to build up your trust balance so that you will accumulate enough equity to cover the challenges that come along. And, once you have cleared the challenges, always remember to resume the habit of making new deposits to build back up the balance in your trust account.

CHAPTER NINE

BUILDING RELATIONSHIPS

"The most important single ingredient in the formula of success is knowing how to get along with people."

–Theodore Roosevelt

I N THE PREVIOUS CHAPTER, WE ESTABLISHED THAT TRUST IS AN essential building block to your success as a manager. In this chapter, we will add five other blocks to help create a solid foundation upon which you will build relationships with your direct reports, peers, and bosses. In fact, the building blocks displayed in the diagramme overleaf are essential for the creation and maintenance of strong, mutually beneficial relationships of all types.

Historically, a false polarity has evolved in the world of work. That false polarity suggests that one has to make a choice between focusing on a task *or* focusing on a relationship. In fact, the choice to be made is not *either* task *or* relationship. Rather, the decision point is about the appropriate levels of focus on task *and* relationship.

Neuroscience experiments conducted by Paul Zak[xiv] found that when people intentionally build social ties at work, their performance improves. This was validated by a Google study which found that managers who express interest in and concern for team members—including their personal wellbeing—outperform their peers in the quality and quantity of their work.

Having established why relationships are so important to your success in your new role, let's take a deeper dive into the five remaining relationship building blocks.

UTDS RELATIONSHIP BUILDING BLOCK MODEL

© Copyright UTDS INC. 2020

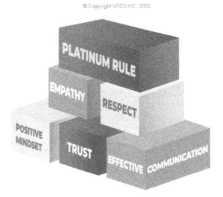

Effective Communication

According to George Bernard Shaw, the single biggest problem in communication is the illusion that it has taken place. In these illusions, one or more party is under the impression that there is shared meaning and understanding. Far too often, this is not the case.

Another factor which contributes to the illusion of communication is the belief that it can be unidirectional—that once you have said or written something, you have communicated. In fact, in the absence of the feedback loop to confirm understanding, there can be no certainty that communication—i.e. the sharing of meaning and understanding—has taken place.

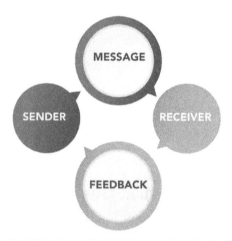

EFFECTIVE COMMUNICATION MODEL

A 2015 study involving 2.5 million work teams in 195 countries found that employee engagement improved when supervisors/managers had some form of daily communication with their direct reports. Based on this finding, we can surmise that both the quality and the quantity of communication correlate positively with favourable business outcomes.

For your feedback loop in the communication cycle to be optimally effective, you need to engage in active listening. Generally speaking, we tend to listen in order to respond. The goal of active listening is understanding—not responding. That shift in purpose has significant implications for how you listen.

In an article published in the *Harvard Business Review* in 2016, Jack Zenger and Joseph Folkman[15] identified four main findings associated with the most effective leaders as identified by 360-degree feedback:

- People perceive the best listeners to be those who periodically ask questions that promote discovery and insight.

---

[15] "What Great Listeners Actually Do" by Jack Zenger and Joseph Folkman (July 14, 2016)

JOAN H. UNDERWOOD

- Good listeners made the other person feel supported by creating a safe environment where issues and differences could be discussed openly.
- Good listening was seen as a cooperative conversation where feedback flowed smoothly in both directions without either party becoming defensive, even when their assumptions or positions were challenged.
- Good listeners provided feedback in a way that opened up new possibilities.

Positive Mindset

Neither individuals nor the relationships we form are static. For this reason, to succeed, we must approach relationships with a positive mindset—i.e. one that is characterised by willingness to explore new possibilities.

According to Mindset.com, mindsets are the "collection of beliefs and thoughts that make up the mental attitude, inclination, habit, or disposition that predetermines a person's interpretations and responses to events, circumstances, and situations." I encourage you to view your mindset as a lens which works in two directions. On the intake side, this lens determines how you "see" and interpret information and situations external to you. On the output side, your lens informs your reasoning and actions. If you change the lens, it could result in a different interpretation and/or different action.

As someone who has worn glasses since I was eleven years old, I can't tell you how many times optometrists have asked me to make a selection between two lenses. The conversation typically goes something like this, "Tell me which one is better—this or this?" as they flip between two lenses in the quest to come up with the prescription that will best enable me to have 20/20 vision. In terms of selecting your mindset, here are some of the binary options you need to make:

- **Open or Closed:** If you adopt an open mindset, you see life from a perspective which believes that people can change. With a closed mindset, you essentially make a judgment call about an individual and reject any notion that they could say or do anything that would cause you to alter your original impression.

- **Learning or Safeguarding**: A learning mindset actively seeks out opportunities to try new things. It acknowledges that making mistakes is part and parcel of the learning process. In contrast, a safeguarding mindset plays it safe by sticking to what is already known and understood. The motivation behind this approach is an aversion to risk.

- **Probing or Steadfast**: Leaders with a probing mindset are inclined to continually seek out new information and approaches. They are on a continuous quest for something better. In contrast, those with a steadfast mindset prefer to stick to what has been tried and proven. For such leaders, good is good enough, and they are likely to resist any change unless a successful outcome can be guaranteed in advance.

- **Promotion or Prevention**: A promotion mindset is oriented towards seeking out gains. The focus is on setting stretch goals and pursuing them relentlessly. In contrast, a prevention mindset is focused on avoiding losses and problems in general.

Awareness of your mindset is part of your emotional intelligence. You will recall that emotional intelligence embodied both self-awareness and self-regulation. In the following chapter, we will explore Situational Leadership and its implications for how you manage the lenses that constitute your mindset.

JOAN H. UNDERWOOD

Respect

Respect begins as an attitude and manifests in behaviour that shows that we consider the other person to be important—that we value and honour them even if we do not agree with them.

While I can assert without fear of contradiction that we all want to be respected, the unfortunate reality is that we don't always treat others with respect. For that reason, I will once again remind you of the Law of the Harvest—we must sow that which we want to reap. If we want to be respected, we must respect others.

You are operating in an increasingly diverse workforce. The factors of diversity are themselves increasing. Today's managers now have to treat with diversity related to age, gender, sexual orientation, race, country of origin, disability, language, etc. Every member of each of those classes wants to maintain their dignity. That aspiration cannot be attained in the absence of respect.

Culture informs what constitutes respect. The norms and cultural mores of Baby Boomers, Millennials, and Gen Xers are quite different. The differences related to race, gender, and nationality can be even more pronounced. Therefore, cultural awareness is part and parcel of this relationship building block. And that brings us to the fifth relationship building block...

Empathy

My favourite definition for empathy comes from the EQ-i 2.0 Model of Emotional Intelligence, which posits that empathy is recognising and appreciating how other people feel. It goes on to state that empathy involves being able to articulate understanding of another's perspective and behaving in a way that respects others' feelings.

Nursing scholar Theresa Wiseman described the following attributes of empathy:

- Ability to take the perspective of another person or to recognise their perspective as their truth;
- Ability to be non-judgmental;
- Ability to recognise emotion in other people; and
- Ability to communicate understanding of another person's feelings.

Each individual has their unique array of knowledge, preferences, beliefs, motivators, stressors, and values which inform their job performance and overall behaviour. To be empathic, you must first acknowledge that the other person's experiences and views of the world are likely to differ from your own—not better or worse, right or wrong; just different.

If you grew up in an individualistic culture (e.g. USA), this could be quite challenging, because such cultures are predisposed to view life from a self-centred perspective. In contrast, the Ubuntu Philosophy,[xv] which originated in Southern Africa, is based on a belief system that honours and celebrates interconnectedness. This is evident in the English translation of ubuntu (Bantu)—"I am because we are."

Once you accept the premise that you are interconnected with the people whom you lead, and that your success as a manager is linked to their success, it then becomes natural for you to be curious about who they are, what they're experiencing, and what they themselves require to succeed.

JOAN H. UNDERWOOD

UTDS EMPATHY MODEL

Seek First To Understand > Then To Be Understood > EMPATHY

© Copyright UTDS INC. 2020

When you approach your relationships from a position of curiosity, you show up with questions rather than answers born out of preconceived notions. You seek first to understand and only then to be understood.

The Platinum Rule

The golden rule, which has its origins in Matthew 7:12, admonishes us to do unto others as we would have them do unto us. This is a well-established Christian principle. However, I put it to you that it is not as effective when applied as a leadership principle. If we treat our direct reports, peers, and bosses as we would like to be treated, we are implying that they are exactly like us, and that they want and value the same things that we do. That is not always a safe or valid assumption.

We all know that the reality is that, while we have certain things in common, we all have our individual preferences and desires. Therefore, perhaps the golden rule is not the best credo. Rather, we have the platinum rule which states, "Do unto others as they would have done unto them." See the difference?

UTDS PLATINUM RULE MODEL

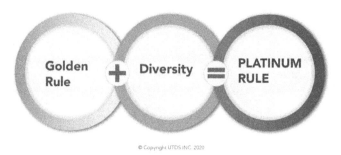

© Copyright UTDS INC. 2020

The platinum rule takes into consideration the significant diversity that exists among human beings. What might the platinum rule mean for the way we interact with our staff and how we go about designing programmes to help them—e.g. programmes to help improve their work-life balance?

During my tenure as an HR Manager for a financial conglomerate several years ago, I realised that the performance incentive programme, which I had designed, was not producing the desired results. Therefore, I decided to conduct a focus group and ask the employees how they would like to be recognised or rewarded. Some of the responses came as a complete surprise to me—e.g. "I'd like to have your executive parking space for a week so that I don't have to drive around in circles every morning looking for parking." Something that I took completely for granted proved to be of great value to many of the staff. And the great thing is that it didn't cost the company a dime for me to honour the request.

What about what it means for how we interact with our peers? Are we frustrated by colleagues who always march to the beat of a different drum? What would happen if we tried to tune into their music/rhythm once in a while instead of always trying to get them to listen to ours?

Is it possible that the difference between the golden rule and the

JOAN H. UNDERWOOD

platinum rule is part of why we don't get the expected/desired results when we organise events/activities for our staff? Could this be why some people are not as grateful/appreciative as we expect them to be when we do things for them? Maybe—just maybe—they're tired of gold and would like to be upgraded to platinum...

 **Application Exercise:**
Communicate Effectively

As with all the other competencies presented in this book, the best way for you to master effective communication is by practising it. As you will recall from Chapter 3 where we examined what's required to build winning habits, it's important to start with small changes. So here's a five-week challenge designed to help you become a more effective communicator.

1. **Week 1**: Pick one of the four behaviours identified by Zenger and Folkman and practice that behaviour in at least two conversations each day. At the end of the day, write down what you did, what you noticed, and what you learned from the exercise.

2. **Week 2**: Pick a second effective listening behaviour and incorporate that along with the behaviour from Week 1 into at least one conversation each day. At the end of the day, write down what you did, what you noticed, and what you learnt from the exercise. NB: This week, you should be using two of the best practice behaviours in each of your practice conversations.

3. **Week 3**: Select a third effective listening behaviour and incorporate that along with the two previously adopted behaviours in at least one conversation each day. NB: You should be

stacking/combining the best practice behaviours—not replacing one with another. At the end of the day, complete the journaling exercise.

4. **Week 4**: During this week, incorporate the final behaviour into your daily conversation so that you are utilizing all four best practice habits. Complete your journaling exercise. This time make note of any specific areas you would like to target for further improvement.

5. **Week 5**: At the beginning of the week, identify three people upon whom you can rely and trust to provide candid feedback. Share with them the areas you would like to improve. Then ask them to monitor your performance throughout the week and give you feedback. Emphasise that this request is to help you develop your skills as an effective communicator. At the end of the week, remember to thank them for providing the feedback.

CHAPTER TEN

SITUATIONAL LEADERSHIP

*There's no such thing as a bad leadership style,
they all work! Leadership is about learning when to
use each style to effectively influence others.*

–Dr. Paul Hershey

Iᴛ's ᴇᴀsʏ ᴛᴏ ʙᴇᴄᴏᴍᴇ ᴏᴠᴇʀᴡʜᴇʟᴍᴇᴅ ʙʏ ᴛʜᴇ ɴᴜᴍʙᴇʀ ᴀɴᴅ ᴄᴏᴍ-plexity of leadership models. As a new manager, you probably have more than enough new things to learn without taking on a slew of leadership theories. What you need is a practical model you can implement. From my experience, the Situational Leadership model fits the bill.

The Situational Leadership model was developed by Dr. Paul Hershey and is almost as old as I am. Its flexibility and efficacy account for its longevity. Instead of a leader-focused, one-size-fits-all approach, it advocates a fit-for-purpose approach based on the individual's ability and willingness to complete the task. Together, ability and willingness constitute an individual's Performance Readiness. It's that level of readiness that informs the extent to which the leader should focus on the task and on the relationship. Let's walk through an example to illustrate the point.

Imagine for a moment that a summer intern has been assigned to your team to help clear a data entry backlog. This is his first job, and he's essentially there because he needs to earn some money to help cover his college expenses in the fall.

Based on the information provided, how would you rate his ability and willingness to complete the data entry assignment? In all likelihood, he doesn't have any specific knowledge and experience related to your organisation's proprietary software or the data to be entered into the system. Therefore, as he starts his internship, his ability is low.

In terms of his willingness, after a semester of working hard, the last-minute submission of term papers and surviving some killer final exams, waking up early every day, and coming into an office to sit in front of a computer and key in data for eight hours is probably not his idea of a fun summer. So, his willingness is probably at the lower end of the chart as well.

Based on that combination of circumstances, you would classify your intern's overall performance readiness as low. Therefore, in order to get the job done, the Situational Leadership model stipulates that the appropriate approach to adopt in this context would be one of telling your intern what to do. In so doing, you would be highly directive and focus primarily on the task with minimal focus on developing a relationship with him at that time.

The scenario I have just outlined translates into quadrant S1 and Performance Readiness R1 in the diagramme below.

JOAN H. UNDERWOOD

SITUATIONAL LEADERSHIP®
Influence Behaviors

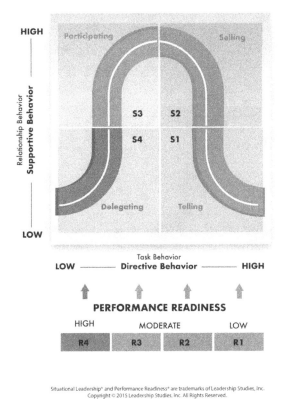

Situational Leadership® and Performance Readiness® are trademarks of Leadership Studies, Inc.
Copyright © 2015 Leadership Studies, Inc. All Rights Reserved.

The following table takes a deeper dive into the model by exploring what constitutes the levels of readiness and how you should show up as a leader in each situation.

Employee's Performance Readiness		Appropriate Leadership Style	
R1	I don't know what to do and am afraid to make a mistake	Telling or Guiding	Leader's focus is on the task. She utilises her knowledge and experience to provide direction, make decisions, and stimulate action.
R2	I'm not sure what to do, but I'm eager to learn.	Selling or Explaining	Leader clarifies the decision-making process to create understanding. Leader acknowledges and encourages enthusiasm.
R3	I have a good under-standing of what to do. I'm just not sure if I'm ready to handle it on my own.	Participating or Involving	Leader engages the em-ployee in problem solving to achieve shared owner-ship of solutions
R4	I am motivated, com-petent, and confident. I got this!	Delegating or Entrusting	Leader creates space and trusts the employee to deliver.

At first glance, this approach to leadership might appear to be some-what complicated. So you might be concerned that it's going to take some time and effort for you to figure out where each of your direct reports is in terms of level of readiness. You might even be thinking that it's proba-bly simpler/easier to just lead everyone the same way, and hope and pray that it will all work out in the end. If that thought resonates with you, don't beat yourself up for it. It's perfectly natural. Unfortunately, it's also perfectly wrong. Trust me, I've tried both approaches!

Here's the thing—if all you have is a screwdriver, you just might walk around treating everything as if it were a screw. That will work like a charm whenever you encounter a screw. However, on those occasions when you encounter a nail or a piece of wood or a hammer, the outcome won't be nearly as satisfying for you or the recipients of the unwanted and unsuitable treatment.

There was a time—long, long ago—when my go-to leadership style was Telling. In my youthful exuberance (and, frankly, ignorance…), I thought I knew what needed to be done and how to do it, and that the most efficient way to proceed was to simply relay that to my direct reports. I expected them to mobilise like good soldiers and execute my master plan. Some complied with my expectations. Others didn't. Overall, the quality of my interpersonal relationships was less than optimal. Additionally, over time I started to become a little resentful that I had to always be the one to come up with solutions. At the same time, those members of the team who were willing and able to do more felt stifled by my one-size-fits-all leadership style. The bottom line is that I was not properly leveraging all the resources I had at my disposal.

So, thinking that I had learnt a lesson, I decided to give my direct reports more autonomy. Problem is that I once again adopted the same style across the board. I started delegating tasks—willy-nilly. Of course, that didn't work either! Some of my direct reports (those who were both willing and able—R4) loved it. However, those who were at R2 or R3 were really stressed out by what they perceived as being thrown into the deep end without a flotation device.

Ultimately, my salvation (and that of my direct reports) came with the realization that leadership really is situational, and that one size truly doesn't fit all.

 ## Application Exercise: Select the Appropriate Leadership Approach

The best way to master this approach to management is to practice it. So let's start that right now.

Think about a task that your team needs to accomplish but which has not yet been assigned to anyone. Assess the ability and willingness of your direct reports to whom the task could possibly be assigned. Use this information to place each eligible direct report in the appropriate quadrant of the Situational Leadership grid.

In the upcoming week or two, utilise the following guide to inform how you interact with each of the selected direct reports as you work with and through them to accomplish the task. At the end of that period, take the time to analyse what transpired. Take note of what worked well and what you think you should have done differently. I also encourage you to consider asking your direct reports for feedback.

- **Quadrant S1: Telling**—Once it's determined that the employee is both unable and unwilling to complete the task, you should be highly directive—focused primarily on the task and less on your relationship with the employee.
- **Quadrant S2: Selling**—Once it's determined that the employee is willing but unable to complete the task, you should focus both on the task and on the relationship with the employee—explaining what needs to be done and how, and encouraging the employee's enthusiasm.
- **Quadrant S3: Participating**—Once it's determined that the employee is able but unwilling to perform the task, you should focus primarily on supporting the employee and building a relationship with them. Explore the reason for the lack of willingness. Listen actively and support them in building up a more positive attitude towards the task.
- **Quadrant 4: Delegating**—Once it's determined that the employee is both willing and able to perform the task, trust them to do the job. This translates to low involvement with

JOAN H. UNDERWOOD

both the task and the relationship as the employee is allowed to operate autonomously with predetermined check-ins and follow up.

As a manager, your aim is to help the members of your team reach their full potential. When this plan comes together and the stars align just right, you get to the point where all the members of your team are both willing and able. At that point, it's time to delegate, which brings us to the next chapter…

CHAPTER ELEVEN

THE ART AND SCIENCE OF DELEGATION

Delegation is the process of passing on responsibility to carry out a specific task, as well as the authority to do so.

ACCORDING TO A 2015 STUDY,[16] 78% OF EMPLOYEES IN MAJOR CORPOrations think their bosses routinely do work that could be effectively delegated to more junior employees. The research also revealed that 66% of managers said they would like to increase their use of delegation as a time management and personnel development tool. Given these statistics, the question then arises—why aren't managers utilising delegation more?

Barriers to Effective Delegation

Common barriers to the effective use of delegation include:

- Perfectionism

---

[16] Statistics presented by Leadership Choice during a June 2015 ATD webinar.

- Time constraints
- Concern that direct reports lack the necessary knowledge or skills
- Being uncomfortable asking for help
- Belief that the project/task is "too important"

Even when managers overcome these barriers, there is a high probability that they will fall prey to one of the many traps of ineffective delegation. Such traps can exist at two extremes of a spectrum—an abdication of responsibility at one end and micromanagement at the other end. Here's how these two extremes show up in the workplace.

Abdication of Responsibility (aka Dump and Run)	Micromanagement/ Over-Engineering
Waits until the last minute to assign tasks	Provides too much lead time, eliminating any sense of urgency
Omits important details about the job	Provides too many details and leaves no room for creativity
Doesn't provide necessary resources	Provides too much information
Assumes the person will "figure things out by themselves"	Tries to answer every question before it's asked
Assigns jobs to people who may not be competent to do them	Assigns jobs to people who are over-qualified and will be bored
Doesn't check in or monitor progress	Doesn't give the employee any breathing room

The sweet spot is somewhere in the middle of these two extremes and involves the following measures:

- Providing enough lead time for the task to be done right
- Sharing relevant facts as well as a "big picture"
- Providing needed resources
- Providing time to ask questions and figure things out
- Assigning jobs to people who are competent to do them
- Letting go, but remaining available to help

- Monitoring progress without micromanaging
- Building confidence and trust with sincere feedback

Ten Commandments for Effective Delegation

Where do you currently stand in the delegation spectrum? Are you of the dump-and-run ilk, or would your direct reports describe you as more of a micromanager? If you currently fall into either of these two extremes, the following ten commandments can enable you to redeem yourself.

10

COMMANDMENTS FOR
GREAT DELEGATION

01 Only delegate when appropriate.

02 Provide context – be clear about what is required and why it is important; link the task to the organisation's visions and objectives.

03 Delegate to the right person – confirm willingness and ability.

04 Delegate authority and responsibility – without the necessary authority, your staff will not be empowered to complete the assigned task.

05 Support don't abdicate – delegation does not mean complete withdrawal; your staff may need training, encouragement, and feedback.

06 Specify the results you want – clearly communicate what would constitute success.

07 Establish the timeframe – ensure that it's realistic and secure agreement.

08 Determine the level of delegated authority – be explicit about how much autonomy the person has to take action and make decisions.

09 Check for consistency and overlaps – clearly communicate which members of the team are responsible for the various elements of the delegated task.

10 Track progress and be available – set up a mutually acceptable reporting and communication system.

© Copyright UYDS INC. 2020

JOAN H. UNDERWOOD

We will now take a deeper dive into each of the ten commandments.

Commandment #1: Only delegate when it's appropriate. Given our working definition of leadership—i.e. getting things done with and through others—delegation is a quintessential leadership competency. However, it has its time and place.

You can use the following decision tree to assess whether to delegate a task. The bottom line is that some tasks are too strategic, too confidential, or too risky for you to hand them off to a subordinate. Having said that, if you find yourself using this decision tree and concluding that there's nothing eligible for delegation, then I encourage you to return to the beginning of this chapter and have a candid conversation with yourself about whether you are putting up unnecessary barriers.

DELEGATION DECISION FLOW CHART

Commandment #2: Provide context. Context truly matters. If you have any doubt about that, I invite you to log onto YouTube and watch *Start with Why* by Simon Sinek.[xvi] With approximately 50 million viewers, it ranks among the top 5 TED Talks of all time. In delegating a task, it is important to communicate why it is important—how it contributes to the departmental or organisational vision and mission. When this information is shared, the person to whom the task is being delegated understands that she is contributing to something bigger than the immediate task—something which has purpose and meaning.

Commandment #3: Delegate to the right person. As indicated during our discussion of Situational Leadership, the person to whom you are delegating a task needs to be ready. In this context, readiness has two components—ability and willingness. When combined, they form a graded scale as illustrated in the diagramme below.

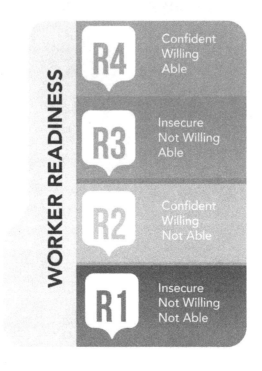

The lowest level of readiness is represented by R1. Individuals in this category are both unable and unwilling to execute the task at hand. Individuals in the R2 category, while willing, are unable to complete the task in that they do not possess the requisite knowledge and/or skills. The converse applies to people who fall into the R3 category. They are able but unwilling to carry out the task in question. The final category is R4. These individuals are both willing and able and, therefore, ideal candidates for delegation.

So, the million-dollar question for you as a new manager is how do you go about determining an individual's level of readiness? The answer to that question lies in a somewhat unattractive acronym— named TOAD.

- **Testing** provides information on the employee's ability
- **Observation** provides information on both ability and willingness
- **Asking** questions can provide insight into both ability and willingness
- **Data** or previously completed work or stats on sales targets can provide tangible proof of the individual's ability or inability

Commandment #4: Delegate authority and responsibility. At this point you have already determined that the individual is both willing and able to execute the task. Therefore, your next move is to get out of their way and allow them to do it. In other words, don't micromanage! Rather, you should facilitate their success by ensuring they have access to the necessary resources to get the job done. I'll illustrate this point with an example of what is likely to happen when you delegate responsibility without the attendant authority.

Several years ago, I had oversight responsibility for the HR function at an all-inclusive hotel resort in Antigua. The front desk staff was responsible for ensuring all guests had a positive experience upon check-in. One night the British Airways flight from London was delayed by several hours. As a result, the guests arrived well close to midnight (Eastern Caribbean Time), having left their homes in the wee hours (GMT), endured hours of waiting at the airport in London, then an eight-hour transatlantic flight, then another few hours clearing immigration and customs and taxi rides to the resort. They were understandably exhausted and famished.

The front desk supervisor—given her responsibility to provide a positive check-in experience for the guests, and anticipating that they would have been hungry—had contacted the kitchen prior to the end of the dinner shift and requested that snacks be prepared for the late arrivals. Unfortunately, the front desk staff did not have the authority to direct the kitchen staff to prepare meals which had not previously been budgeted. As a result, the kitchen staff declined to fulfil the request.

So, let this be a cautionary tale for you. Always remember to delegate both responsibility and the authority required to get the job done.

Commandment #5: Support, don't abdicate. By now, I trust that you're sold on the idea that micromanagement is not the way to go. However, it's equally important that you don't swing to the other end of the spectrum. For a reminder of what that looks like, please have another look at the table presented earlier in this chapter.

Commandment #6: Specify the results you want. It's easy to assume that your staff will understand what you expect from them. As it turns out, there are few mind readers in the workplace. Therefore, rather than assuming, it's important that you explicitly communicate your expectations, including quality standards and anything that's ruled out as a course of action for getting the job done.

Commandment #7: Establish the timeframe. This is actually an extension of the previous commandment. Be explicit in terms of how soon you expect the delegated task to be completed. So, if you're delegating the drafting of a report, stipulate when you expect to receive the draft. In setting the timeline, remember to allow time in the event that revisions are required before you have to submit the report to the end user.

Commandment #8: Determine the level of delegated authority. We touched on the importance of delegating authority when we covered Commandment #4. This Commandment expands on that principle by highlighting the fact that there are varying levels of authority. By establishing at the onset the level of autonomy being conferred on your direct report, you can minimise the likelihood of misunderstanding.

The assigned level of authority can fall into three categories based on variables, including your own comfort level. What's most important is that the assigned level is clearly articulated and understood and accepted by both parties. Here are your three options:

- Level 1: employee is expected to recommend a course of action to complete the task and submit same to you for approval prior to implementation;
- Level 2: employee is expected to utilise his best judgment and take independent action, and then immediately update you on what was done; or
- Level 3: employee is authorised to take independent action and update you during routine procedures or reporting cycles.

Establishing this level of specificity at the onset is a valuable tool to help fend off the temptation to micromanage.

Commandment #9: Check for consistency and overlaps. This commandment is particularly important when you are working on a project or other venture which has interdependencies. The previous example involving the front desk and kitchen staff at the hotel is a case in point. While the front desk had been assigned responsibility for providing an exceptional check-in experience for guests, the kitchen staff had been assigned responsibility to reduce expenditures. The scenario in question represented conflicting priorities.

In your role as manager, you have an obligation to survey the terrain to identify potential obstacles to the successful execution of the delegated task. Having identified any such obstacles, your next step is to remove or at least mitigate their adverse impact. In some instances, this might require notifying other employees about the assigned task and soliciting their assistance. This is particularly important when the execution of the assigned functions requires collaboration across departments or units which are outside of your direct chain of command.

Commandment #10: Track progress and be available. This final commandment is closely aligned with Commandments #5 and #8. One of the most effective ways of supporting your direct report is to maintain open communication lines and letting them know you're available if and when the need arises. So, in addition to the reporting protocols you established under Commandment #8, it's important to let your direct report know they can come to you if they encounter any unanticipated difficulties. Caveat: Resist the temptation to reclaim the task if they do come to you to discuss a challenge. Remember, you've already established that the individual is both willing and able. What's required of you in that context is to provide support—not to send them back to the bench while you take over. Doing so could lead to an erosion of trust in the relationship.

CHAPTER TWELVE

GIVING AND RECEIVING FEEDBACK

"Please know that honest feedback is more valuable than positive feedback. If you really want to see someone raise their game, you will tell them what they need to hear... not what they want to hear."

–Alan Stein Jr.[xvii]

IN THIS CHAPTER WE FOCUS BOTH ON GIVING AND RECEIVING FEEDBACK. In your new role as manager, these two competencies are equally important. Did you notice that I referred to both as competencies? That was very deliberate. There is a right and a wrong way to do both, and you need to practice to become proficient.

To help you master these competencies, I will address the following questions:

- What is the purpose of feedback?
- When is the right time for feedback?

- Who should provide feedback?
- Where should feedback be provided?
- How should feedback be structured?

Giving Feedback

Purpose: One of your primary responsibilities as a manager is to help the members of your team realise their full potential. This requires that you give them feedback on their performance. Such feedback can be divided into two categories—that which provides positive reinforcement and serves to build their confidence, and that which is developmental and helps them to close performance gaps.

Right Time: Since the purpose of feedback is to improve future performance, it follows that feedback should be given in a timely manner. It should be close enough to the event that both you and your direct report can recall what transpired. It should be immediate enough that it serves to influence future performance (in the case of developmental feedback) and to boost confidence and enhance the likelihood of repeat performance (in the case of positive reinforcement).

I had an epic fail in this regard when I took up my first bona fide managerial position. I recruited someone to serve as my second-in-command. On paper, he checked all the right boxes. However, as his probation period advanced, I became more and more frustrated by what I perceived as a lack of initiative and inadequate attention to detail. I kept expecting him to get it right and continued to be disappointed when he didn't. I eventually decided that I could not confirm him in the position but would terminate at the end of the probationary period.

I remember sitting him down to deliver the bad news. To my surprise, he appeared blindsided by my decision. I wondered how on earth did he not realise that I was not pleased with his performance? After all, did he not remember how many times I had asked him to redo tasks? I painstakingly rehashed the instances of missed deadlines, lack of initiative, overlooked details, etc. At the end of my litany, he looked genuinely bemused and asked me a question that I was hard pressed to answer: "Why didn't you point all this out to me before so that I could have had a chance to fix it?"

Upon careful reflection, I had to concede that I had failed to live up to my responsibility to provide timely feedback to my assistant manager. My failure deprived him of the opportunity to address the performance gaps during his probationary period. My takeaway from that epic fail was that to be effective, feedback must be timely. Delaying it deprives the individual of the opportunity to improve. It also deprives the organisation from the benefit of a higher level of performance.

Right Person: When it comes to your direct reports, *you* are the one who should be providing feedback on their performance. As I have stated before (probably so many times that I'm at risk of sounding like a stuck record...), leadership is about getting things done with and through others. You have been assigned to lead a team. You are both responsible and accountable for the performance of that team. Therefore, the onus is on you to commend your team members when they meet or exceed expectations, and to coach them when they do not.

Where: Conventional wisdom holds that you should praise in public and critique in private. At the risk of surprising you, I'm going to buck conventional wisdom—sort of... I absolutely agree that you should never deliver developmental feedback in the presence of an audience. That could serve to erode—or destroy—trust as it could be a source of embarrassment for the person on the receiving end of the feedback. However, some individuals are equally uncomfortable with receiving positive feedback in public.

I recall an incident with one of my direct reports when I served as an HR manager for a financial conglomerate. This particular lady was quiet and unassuming. She had a fantastic eye for detail and actually revelled in completing tasks which most others would find mundane, repetitive, and downright boring. I assigned her to be our primary payroll administrator. She was required to complete separate payroll runs for each of the entities in the conglomerate. She routinely did so on time and error free. This continued as we transitioned to new payroll software. Her aptitude was such that the application provider singled her out to me and mentioned to me that he was quite impressed.

I was delighted to share that positive feedback during our next team meeting. After the meeting, she came to me and pointed out that I had made her uncomfortable by showering her with praise in the presence of the other members of the team. When I asked how she would have liked me to handle it, she indicated that she would have preferred a personal note. I promised to be mindful of that preference going forward.

I had occasion to write a few such notes as time elapsed. Then one day, I noticed that she had them all pinned to the cork board above her workstation. The ink had actually faded on some of them, but it was apparent that, to her, they were cherished possessions.

The most effective managers adjust their leadership style to accommodate the needs of individual employees. The platinum rule— i.e. do unto others as they would like to have done unto them—is another reminder to take diversity into consideration in your interactions with others. So, as you establish your relationships with each of your direct reports, why not simply ask them where and how they

JOAN H. UNDERWOOD

would like to receive performance feedback. I'll wager a bet that they will appreciate that you asked the question.

How: If you remember one thing about the how of giving effective feedback, please let it be this: be specific! Folks, telling someone that they did a good job is *not* effective feedback. What exactly was it about their performance that attracted your commendation? If you aren't specific, it makes it more difficult for the person receiving the feedback to know what they should replicate.

Next, I exhort you to avoid commenting on an individual's personality. For the most part, our personalities are already formed when we enter the world of work. Additionally, most of us actually like ourselves—including our personalities. Therefore, negative comments about an individual's personality are likely to elicit resentment and erode the quality of the relationship. Instead your feedback should focus on behaviour or performance—objectively verifiable information rather than opinions or subjective perspectives.

The final component that I would like to highlight is to outline the impact of the behaviour or performance. You can do this by linking the performance to the departmental goals and objectives. If the feedback is in the form of positive reinforcement, highlight how the employee's performance helped the department to achieve its goals and objectives. If the feedback is about a performance gap, explain the adverse impact associated with the tardiness, errors, cost overrun, etc.

Receiving Feedback

As mentioned in Chapter 1, self-awareness and self-regulation are essential components of emotional intelligence (EI), which is the most valid and reliable predictor of leadership success. According to

Warren Bennis,[xviii] EI accounts for as much as 85 to 90% of success at work. One way to improve your EI is by soliciting feedback.

Purpose: The feedback you receive can help to bring information from your unknown to known area. You can then proceed to change the narrative as required to better align with the image you want to portray.

Right Time: Since feedback is geared towards helping you enhance your performance, the best time to get it is as soon as possible. When you secure feedback in close proximity to the behaviour/performance, it enables you to respond in real time to either reinforce current behaviour, or rectify negative behaviour or performance.

Right Person: While you don't have absolute control of who provides feedback on your performance as a new manager, you can certainly give yourself a leg up by proactively building a network of trusted peers and seniors upon whom you can rely to be candid with you.

You may have noticed that I didn't include your direct reports in the list of people eligible for inclusion in your feedback network. The power imbalance inherent in your relationship with your direct reports might make them reluctant to share negative feedback or raise problematic issues with you. However, there is a way that you can mitigate that risk.

Once you have utilised the six relationship building blocks presented in Chapter 9, that solid foundation could provide a platform for your direct reports to feel safe giving you candid feedback. To create and maintain that safety, you will need to establish a reputation for being open to such feedback and reacting calmly. Above all, you will need to ensure that you do not develop a reputation for holding a grudge—even when the feedback you receive is not complimentary.

Several years ago, I was conducting my first performance appraisal for my second-in-command. My practice was to have each direct report complete a self-assessment and then we would sit together and compare the ratings. There was a particular responsibility for which I had assigned a rating of below expectations. She met or exceeded expectations in all other areas. She was not at all pleased with my rating, and she made that known!

I presented the data which informed my rating. In turn, she explained why she thought the data in question should be attributed to extenuating circumstances and therefore not factor into her rating. We had a lively debate, which ended with my maintaining my original assessment. I could tell she was profoundly disappointed. However, she earned my respect when she ended the meeting with the statement: "I promise you that you will never again have the opportunity to tell me that my performance is below expectations!"

Our formal work relationship continued for about six years after that incident. And she was absolutely right! In fact, it's been over fifteen years, and I still routinely collaborate with her as a subcontractor on major consulting assignments, and in each and every instance, she meets or exceeds my expectations.

Where: As I mentioned when discussing the appropriate place to give feedback, it depends. I encourage you to identify what works best for you and to share that information with your trusted network.

How: Not everyone who will have occasion to give you feedback would have read this book or otherwise been exposed to relevant best practices. Therefore, the onus may be on you to ask the right questions to get feedback that is most helpful to you.

Here are a few tips:

- If feedback is not readily forthcoming, ask for it.
- If the feedback received is kind of fuzzy, ask the individual if they could please be more specific.

- If the feedback you receive is focused on your attitude or personality, politely ask the person if they could please give you an example of the specific behaviour so that you can better understand their concerns and take appropriate action.
- Ask for advice on steps that you could take to address the performance gaps that have been identified.
- If you need help to close a performance gap, don't be afraid to reach out and ask for it.

Job Aid: Effective Feedback

The following job aid is designed to help you master the competency of giving and receiving effective feedback.

Benefits of Giving Effective Feedback

- People get clear about the impact of their behaviour and what is expected of them.
- It promotes curiosity and encourages others to try new behaviours.
- Giving effective feedback is a respectful way to help another person succeed. (If you can't discuss it, you can't improve it.)
- Feedback is the most powerful tool available to shape another's behaviour; the best way to do this is to "catch people doing something right" and then reinforce it.

Effective Feedback Can Be Used To:

- Honour competence and reinforce desired behaviour
- Help align expectations and priorities
- Fill gaps in knowledge
- Let people know where to take corrective action
- Alleviate fear of the unknown

JOAN H. UNDERWOOD

When Giving Feedback:

- Link to departmental purpose/goals
- Focus on the future
- Put it in context (how severe?)
- Be specific
- Make it timely
- Focus on behaviour, not personality
- Explain the impact
- Speak from the heart—be sincere and authentic
- Speak for yourself—i.e. don't say "people say..."
- Don't inflict feedback. Remember: it's a developmental tool—not punishment.

Hard-Won Wisdom—What Life Has Taught Me

- Intention is as important as technique or content. Be certain your intention is to help or appreciate.
- Delayed feedback loses impact. Be FAST: **F**requent, **A**ccurate, **S**pecific, **T**imely.
- Feedback is not Truth. It is another's perception. When you receive unsettling feedback, stay curious. Ask questions. Seek to understand before defending or problem solving.
- As a manager, avoiding giving feedback to an employee who is not performing undermines your credibility and may send a message that mediocrity or bad behaviour will be tolerated.
- Leaders who give and solicit honest and respectful feedback model courage and humility.

CHAPTER THIRTEEN

HOW TO PERSUADE AND INFLUENCE

*"The ability to connect and influence
people, that's the job of a leader."*
–Tony Robbins

L EADERSHIP IS ALL ABOUT GETTING THINGS DONE WITH AND through others. In a bygone era, managers utilised command and control measures to accomplish this. Today, effective leaders have a much more expansive toolkit, and they are well aware the old, authoritarian approach to leadership generally produces suboptimal results, and definitely is not the way to leverage the discretionary effort routinely deployed by highly engaged employees.

Robert Cialdini[xix] is the acknowledged guru in the field of persuasion and influence. In his bestselling book *Influence: The Psychology of Persuasion*, he presents six universal principles which, if effectively utilised, can help you to master the essential skills of persuasion and influence.

Liking

In 2019, C-Span commissioned a team of experts to adjudicate who was the best president in the history of the United States of America. The panellists were required to rank each president based on factors such as public persuasion, crisis leadership, international relations, and vision. The winner was Abraham Lincoln, affectionately known as Honest Abe.

Lincoln, who served as the 16th President of the USA, and who led that country through the Civil War and initiated the abolition of slavery, is quoted to have stated: *"If you wish to win a man over to your ideas, first make him your friend."*

That advice from Lincoln is consistent with Robert Cialdini's Principle of Liking, which posits that people like those who like them. It also reinforces what we covered in our earlier discussion of Trust. Benevolence and character are essential components of what renders a person trustworthy. In turn, trustworthiness is fundamental to likability.

So, how can you capitalise on this in your new role as manager? To start, be guided by the fact that people tend to like those with whom they have something in common. Therefore, actively seek to identify things you have in common with your direct reports, peers, bosses, and anyone else with whom you interact.

Reciprocity

In Chapter 8, we spoke about the Law of the Harvest as it relates to trust. The principle is that you sow what you would like to reap. The validity of this principle is grounded in the fact that human beings are predisposed to reciprocate or repay in kind. Therefore, effective leaders model the behaviour they would like to see in their team.

During the first quarter of 2020, I was facilitating an executive development programme at the Cave Hill School of Business/University of the West Indies. The participants were military and paramilitary leaders from throughout the Caribbean. I delivered a lecturette on Cialdini's principles of persuasion. The circumstances surrounding President Donald Trump's recent impeachment proved to be fodder for a very lively discussion about the difference between reciprocity and quid pro quo. I relate that story here, because it is a distinction that is very important for you to appreciate as a leader.

President Trump's articles of impeachment stipulate that he conditioned two official acts on the Ukrainian government's complying with his request to make certain public announcements. The requested announcements were deemed to be in his personal political interests. The conditionality is what removed the president's actions from the realm of reciprocity and planted it squarely in the realm of manipulation.

To further illustrate the distinction, I turn to another geopolitical example—this one involving Trinidad and Tobago and the People's Republic of China. When news first broke of the Novel Coronavirus epidemic in Wuhan, China, the Caribbean island nation of Trinidad and Tobago donated 15,000 surgical masks to help the global superpower in its fight against the deadly virus.

Not too long thereafter, the World Health Organization (WHO) would declare Covid-19 a pandemic, and Trinidad and Tobago would find itself waging battle against the deadly virus. The Government of China then donated 4,000 viral test kits (at a time when there was a global shortage of said kits), 15 sets of body temperature systems, and a supply of personal protective equipment.

There was no conditionality associated with the initial gift. Rather, it was a show of support to a friendly nation in a time of hardship or challenge. In keeping with the Law of the Harvest, that altruistic gesture yielded much fruit in due course.

Scarcity

Cialdini points out that the feeling of being in competition for scarce resources has powerfully motivating properties. This particular principle has great utility in marketing, which was the focus of Dr. Cialdini's groundbreaking research. Knowing that there is limited access to a product or service can help to stimulate demand for said product or service. The bottom line is that people tend to want more of what they can have less of—hence the frequent and effective use of phrases such as limited-time offer, limited quantities available, exclusive offer, etc.

Outside of the sales and marketing context, I advise extreme discretion in the use of this particular principle. The imprudent use of the Scarcity Principle in a team setting could serve to alienate some members and to create the impression that you are promoting a tiered system rather than an equitable one. In situations where you want to promote collaboration—rather than competition—the scarcity principle should be deployed with caution.

Authority

People tend to defer to experts. Therefore, it's important for you to establish your expertise and authority in your new role. This can prove to be a challenge for women because of the way we may have been socialised.

Growing up, my grandmother always told me that self-praise was no kind of praise. In other words, it was better to have others sing your praises rather than to do so yourself. That lesson became ingrained in me. As a result, when I met my husband and he began extolling his accomplishments in sports and various other endeavours, I expressed scepticism born out of my acceptance of my grandmother's words of caution. Without missing a beat, my husband inquired who could possibly be better suited to blow his trumpet than he himself... That conversation ultimately led me to reconsider my perspective.

My grandmother was not the only social influence suggesting that it wasn't becoming for girls/women to self-promote. Research into the attitude of male versus female job applicants has shown that women tend not to apply for a job unless they think they have met *all* of the requirements. And, even when describing their accomplishments, they tend to use language that downplays rather than emphasises individual accomplishments and competitive spirit. In contrast, men are more willing to apply for jobs for which they are not fully qualified, and to overstate the extent of their relevant experience.

Whatever your gender, what the authority principle advocates is that you send an unequivocal message that you are competent and possess the relevant expertise to get the job done. The onus is on you to inspire confidence in those you seek to lead. Of course, it is helpful when others sing your praises. Therefore, I encourage you to develop relationships with mentors and sponsors who can assist you with this. However, in the spirit of taking ownership of your professional development, you simply cannot afford to abdicate your responsibility to blow your own horn—just ensure that it's properly tuned so that you can carry the tune well!

Consistency

For the most part, people want to be perceived as being consistent—as opposed to wishy-washy or as someone who is always vacillating or whose word cannot be trusted. This is something you can use to your advantage when seeking to influence behaviour, since someone who has made an explicit commitment is more likely to feel bound to honour it.

JOAN H. UNDERWOOD

Let's imagine for a moment you have a direct report whose error rates are outside of the performance standards you have established. During a performance management meeting with him, you brainstorm steps he can take to address the issue. One way you can concretise the improvement plan is to task him with writing it up and submitting it to you. The act of committing the performance improvement measures to paper serves as a powerful motivator for him to implement the agreed-upon changes.

This principle can also be applied at the team level by developing a team charter and having all members sign off on same. We will cover team charters in depth in Chapter 15. For now, suffice it to say, such charters are a powerful tool for securing accountability within the team.

There is a significant caveat related to the use of the consistency principle. If the individual(s) feels that you forced them to make the public undertaking or commitment, it will not have the same binding effect. Therefore, you are strongly encouraged to resist the temptation to resort to the use of threats or coercion to secure compliance. Doing so creates the opportunity for the individual to renege and to accuse you of having manipulated them into agreeing to something against their will.

Social Proof

Whether we are willing to admit it or not, humans are social beings. We exist in communities and are influenced by those around us. That influence is more pronounced in times of uncertainty when we look to others and gauge their reaction as part of the process of formulating our own actions.

While the term peer pressure tends to have a negative connotation, astute leaders can leverage peer power as part of their strategy to persuade and influence others. For example, if you or your organisation want to implement a major change initiative, clearly you will be an advocate for said initiative. However, an additional strategy you could deploy would be to identify peer champions within your team. The individuals selected should enjoy the trust and respect of their colleagues. They should also be genuinely convinced of the merit of the proposed change and able to speak to both the pros and cons in a way that is authentic and inspires confidence.

The efficacy of social proof is evident in the popularity of personal testimonies as a tool for promoting everything from religion to a particular brand. Perhaps it even played a role in your decision to purchase this book...

I cannot end this chapter without a word of caution about the difference between persuasion and manipulation. In the words of Simon Sinek,[17] "[there are] two ways to influence human behaviour: you can manipulate it or you can inspire it." The six principles outlined by Dr. Cialdini are meant to be used for good. However, some leaders cross the threshold from persuasion to manipulation, which are both ways of exerting influence. The difference is a matter of intent. It comes down to ethics in terms of whether you use your powers for good or bad. In making that determination, I encourage you to remember the Law of the Harvest—don't sow seeds whose fruit would likely set your teeth on edge!

---

[17] Simon Sinek, *Start with Why: How Great Leaders Inspire Everyone to Take Action*

JOAN H. UNDERWOOD

CHAPTER FOURTEEN

MANAGING YOUR BOSS

"When your boss listens to you carefully, reaches out to help you, and learns from you, it enhances your dignity and pride. Doing so also helps your boss gain empathy for you, to better understand how it feels to be you and what you need to succeed in your job and life."

– Robert I. Sutton[xx]

ABOUT TWENTY YEARS AGO I FOUND MYSELF IN A BIT OF A CO-nundrum. I had just concluded a fixed-term contract, during which I managed a special project for a group of companies operating in the financial services and hospitality sectors. I left a permanent position as a general manager for another company to take on that assignment. Since my friends and family knew that I tended to be risk averse, the decision puzzled many and alarmed more than a few. (Anyway, that's a story for another day and another book...) As I sat in the Managing Director's (MD) office for what could probably be described as my exit interview, he made me an offer that I was tempted to refuse.

After commending me for the way I had designed and executed the special project, the MD indicated he had another assignment for me. He wanted me to come on board to set up an HR Department to service the five companies in the group. Me? HR? At that time I was a generalist with something that fell well short of even a passing interest in HR. Had I been tasked with making a list of the top 20 jobs I'd like to hold, nothing even remotely related to HR would have made the list. Yet, there I was—the only thing standing between me and unemployment was an offer to take up an HR position—and not just any HR position, but one which would require me to build out an entire HR Department to replace a personnel department where the primary functions were payroll and calculating sick leave and vacation entitlements. Uughh!

In the following weeks, I wracked my brain to figure out how I could make this work for me. How could I give the MD what he needed while getting what I wanted? And what was it that I wanted? To be able to do something other than HR! Well, what on the surface might seem to be a problem without a solution turned into a dream job that kept me happy and professionally fulfilled for the next seven years.

Here's how that happened. In the follow-up meeting, I asked the MD to identify the three most important things he wanted/needed me to accomplish in the new role. Once he had outlined them, I realised I could probably deliver all three objectives. Having made that determination, I told him I would take the job and guarantee his three objectives if he, in turn, would amend the job offer to include the following three concessions:

1. Instead of being appointed as the HR Manager, I would be appointed to a role I would design and which would carry the title Manager HR and Strategic Development.

JOAN H. UNDERWOOD

2. Instead of the job being a permanent position, I would sign a three-year contract, during which time I would be required to deliver the three objectives the MD had identified.
3. At the end of that three-year contract, in the event that I decided to stay on with the organisation, I would be relieved of the HR function and would focus on strategic development.

I should also mention that I assured the MD that if I didn't deliver his three objectives, that would be the end of our working relationship. After some negotiations, he accepted my counter-proposal, and I went on to serve as Manager HR and Strategic Development for seven and a half years. It turns out that I fell in love with HR and decided to stick with it.

I've shared that story with you to highlight the importance of managing up. Due to the inherent power imbalance in your relationship with your boss, you may be tempted to overlook the fact that your boss *needs* you—or at least they need someone on whom they can depend to get the job done. I leveraged that knowledge to negotiate a contract that enabled both of us to achieve our goals.

Here are the takeaways from my experience that you can use to establish mutual respect in your relationship with your own boss:

Establish Mutual Expectations: You probably intuitively understand that it's important for you to know what the boss wants from you. However, it's equally important for you to let the boss know what you need from them in order for you to be able to fulfil their expectations. By the way, please don't make the mistake of thinking that the things you need are restricted to a budget and a particular number of employees. You also need to articulate intangible requirements such as communication, access, delegated authority to go along with assigned responsibilities, etc. You take a terrible risk when you assume that it's obvious.

Know and Understand the Boss: Invest the necessary time and effort in getting to know and understand your boss, their work preferences, their strengths and weaknesses, etc.

Between 2009 and 2011, I worked as the Chief Implementation Officer in the Office of the Prime Minister of Antigua and Barbuda. PM Spencer recruited me to help ensure his priority agenda didn't get stuck in the pipelines of government bureaucracy.

With a country to run in the midst of a global financial crisis, my boss was insanely busy. So, for me to add value rather than be a drain on his time and mental energy, I had to ensure that I understood his communication preferences, how he liked to receive information, and what was his decision-making process. That understanding enabled me to increase both the effectiveness and efficiency of my interactions with him. That, in turn, meant that I knew my requests for face-to-face time with him would receive priority attention.

In fact, the ladies in the secretariat frequently commented that the PM always seemed to have time to squeeze me in. The reality is that I made it my business to ensure I added value in each interaction—either by tailoring it to advance his agenda, or to alert him to upcoming pitfalls or obstacles and advise on steps to mitigate same.

Live Up to Your Commitments: Your boss doesn't have the time nor inclination to clean up after you. Therefore, when they are relying on you to get something done, do it! My first indoctrination with this principle came from eleven years of Catholic school. It was one of the many lessons I learnt in childhood that have served me well throughout life.

The words that were drummed into me by the nuns and lay

JOAN H. UNDERWOOD

teachers at the Christ the King High School would later be reinforced when I read *The Four Agreements* by Don Miguel Ruiz.[18] The first agreement simply states, "Be impeccable with your word."

It's Not About You

Sometimes we don't win the good boss jackpot. Whatever hand you're dealt, it's important you know how to play it as skilfully as possible. If you have a good-to-average boss, and you apply the lessons I've outlined thus far, you should be well positioned to succeed. However, if you end up with a boss with whom you have a more challenging relationship, there is still hope.

Everyone shows up in the workplace as a product of their individual personalities and life experiences. And that combination doesn't always turn out pretty. Depending on your own personality and level of self-confidence, encountering a bad boss could prove to be a blow to your ego and could be the source of incredible levels of stress.

Over twenty years ago, I found myself working for a boss who would be eligible to have his jersey retired with full honours by the society of bad bosses—if such a society existed. I was struggling mightily to figure out how to establish a positive working relationship with him. As I struggled, a colleague bought me a particular book and told me to read it so that I would finally stop beating myself up about the contentious nature of my relationship with my boss. The book in question was *Conduct Unbecoming: The Rise and Ruin of Finley Kumble.*[xxi] I discovered that the book documents the flawed nature of my boss's moral compass.

If ever you find yourself in a similar position, I encourage you to step back, take a breath, and say to yourself, "This is not about me!"

---

[18] In this New York Times Bestseller, the author reveals the source of self-limiting beliefs that rob us of joy and create needless suffering.

If your bad boss isn't notorious enough to have had a book written about him, you might get the breakthrough you need by reading *The Four Agreements* by Don Miguel Ruiz. In the Second Agreement, we are admonished not to take anything personally.

"Nothing other people do is because of you. It is because of themselves. All people live in their own dream, in their own mind; they are in a completely different world from the one we live in.

You are never responsible for the actions of others; you are only responsible for you. When you truly understand this, and refuse to take things personally, you can hardly be hurt by the careless comments or actions of others."

How to Make Difficult People Disappear

I know from my own painful experience that, while realizing that it's not about me provides a measure of relief, it's not enough to eliminate all the stress associated with having to deal with a bad boss on a daily basis. That's why I continued to look around for strategies to make my difficult boss disappear.

My breakthrough came when I discovered Monica Wofford's[xxii] book *Make Difficult People Disappear: How to Deal with Stressful Behavior and Eliminate Conflict*. The process of making a bad boss disappear starts with you and not with them. The bottom line is that only you can manage your expectations. Once we stop expecting someone to live according to our own moral compass and behavioural preferences, we can liberate ourselves from getting stressed out each and every time they don't live up to our expectations.

Wofford used the metaphor of different breeds of dogs. All dog lovers are aware that different breeds have different dispositions. For years, I had at least one Doberman in my household. I absolutely adored that regal breed for their devotion, protective drive, and beauty. If one of my Dobies barked, I knew something was happening that required my attention. Then, one day, my sister gifted me with a small white dog that yapped incessantly. In the beginning that frustrated the heck out of me! Why couldn't it be more like my Dobies?

Once I acknowledged that Blanco was not a Dobie and that it was ridiculous for me to expect her to act like one, I came to love and appreciate her for what she brought to the table—for one thing, she loved to cuddle and fit perfectly in my lap. And voilà—my frustration disappeared, and I no longer viewed her as difficult.

Once I made a conscious decision to shift my expectations, Blanco and I got along a lot better. Unfortunately, the Dobies never quite warmed up to their little sister.

So, if your boss is rubbing you the wrong way, rather than researching magic potions to make them disappear, I encourage you to explore how you can shift your expectations. Pair that with empathy and the other essential relationship building blocks from Chapter 9, and you could find yourself well on the way to managing up in a way that minimises your stress and positions you to succeed in your new role.

PART III
MANAGING SYSTEMS & PROCESSES

CHAPTER FIFTEEN

BUILDING A HIGH-PERFORMANCE TEAM

"Trust is a MUST in high-performance teams, because without trust we cannot fully collaborate. We just cooperate to keep our jobs, instead of creating exponential results. It is the shift from fear and protection, to trust and love, that activates, unleashes, and aligns, the fullest team potentials."

– Tony Dovale[xxiii]

IT IS IMPORTANT TO ACKNOWLEDGE THAT NOT ALL TEAMS ARE high-performance teams. In many instances, what exists would be more aptly described as a work group. Traditional work groups are organised around functions; employees do specialised tasks; people are viewed as tools of management; the group is governed by rules, and everything is overseen by a supervisor/manager. If this describes your work environment, then you are probably operating in a work group.

There is nothing inherently wrong with work groups. They can be effective in executing their mandate. However, high-performance teams represent a higher level of evolution compared to the traditional work group. In case you are wondering how you can determine if you have a high-performance team, here is a checklist you can use:

- ✓ A clear vision
- ✓ Universal commitment to the vision
- ✓ Clearly articulated strategy for achieving the vision
- ✓ Established performance indicators
- ✓ Effective monitoring and evaluation
- ✓ Open communication and positive relationships
- ✓ Effective problem identification and resolution systems
- ✓ Established decision-making protocols
- ✓ Effective conflict resolution
- ✓ Shared leadership responsibilities
- ✓ Productive meetings
- ✓ Clearly defined roles and work procedures
- ✓ Cross-functional cooperation

In this chapter, we will explore the building blocks required to create a high-performance team. In doing so, I will draw on my experiences leading such a team—a team which was responsible for the HR function in a financial conglomerate. It so happens that we were an all-female team. However, that is not a pre-requisite. The dynamic we achieved can be replicated by any team as long as the members remain steadfastly committed to the principles I am about to outline.

With express permission from Brendalie, Blanka, Oneka, Emarline, Kerry, and Patsy, I will be sharing with you some of our many successes as well as our opportunities for learning. I pay tribute to these ladies individually and collectively and owe them a debt of gratitude for the role they played in helping me to become a better leader.

I cannot pinpoint the day when we transitioned from being a traditional work group to a high-performance team. However, there is no doubt in any of our minds that that is exactly what we became, although we never quite articulated it that way at that time. We only realised how remarkable our team was years later as we compared our history together to our experiences in other roles and/or other organisations.

As you take this journey with us, it is important you remember the lead quote from Tony Dovale and its emphasis on the importance of trust. None of the successes of my high-performance HR team could have been realised in the absence of a bedrock of mutual trust and genuine love—both of which continue today, almost a decade after our formal working relationship came to an end.

Creating a Team Charter

"A team charter can help create energy, focus, and buy-in from members joining your team, or it can help recharge a team that has been in existence for a long time, but needs to regroup and refocus."
—Smartsheet.com[19]

I'm sure you've heard the saying, "If you don't know where you're going, any road will get you there." Well, if you don't have a team charter, not only do you not know where you're going, but you also don't know if you're getting there by plane, boat, car, or high-speed train. A team charter helps to unite members around the what, why, and how of its operations.

While there are many models/templates that you can use to create your team charter, the one that has worked best for me over the years answers five simple questions.

---

[19] Excerpt from "The Essential Guide to Creating an Effective Team Charter"

Question #1: To whom are you accountable?

In response to this question, you and your team should create a list of your key customers and stakeholders. Notice that I said this is an exercise you should complete with the members of your team. Involving them in the crafting of the team charter will help to secure a sense of ownership and commitment.

As you brainstorm the answer to this question, it's possible that the list might become quite lengthy. If that is the case, I recommend that you document all the responses and then go through a process of prioritising based on who will be most impacted by your team's work or those who will be relying most heavily on your team's outputs.

Question #2: What are you expected to accomplish?

Once you have created your priority list of customers and stakeholders, you and your team should then ask yourselves what each of those customers or stakeholders expects you to produce or deliver. You need to be specific in answering this question. For example, instead of saying "good service," you should be explicit in terms of what would constitute good service. Stipulated parameters include considerations such as cost, timeliness/speed, quality, and quantity.

Question #3: Why does the team exist?

Separate and apart from the products or services your team generates, it has a larger purpose—a reason for existing. You and your team need to define that purpose and check to ensure it resonates with your key stakeholders and customers.

Having a compelling why helps to promote team focus and enthusiasm. Your purpose statement should have two components—firstly, the contribution you make; and secondly, the impact that said contribution is intended to have.

For example, Apple® exists to challenge the status quo. They do this by thinking differently. As a result of this purpose, they are known for their innovation and focus on customer experience and have secured a high level of customer loyalty.

> *"Those who are clear on their why are the ones who have never given up and have succeeded." —Simon Sinek*[xxiv]

Question #4: What kind of team do you want to be?

While having your team's identity evolve is an option, if you want to create a high-performance team, you need to be more mindful and deliberate. One way to accomplish this is to work with your staff to identify the characteristics of your (i.e. the collective) ideal team. One way to get the conversation going is to ask your staff to think about the best and worst teams they know. You can then use the results of that exercise to decide what you want your team to be and what you definitely don't want it to be.

In making this determination, it may be helpful to use a sporting metaphor to illustrate the different types of teams. The two determinant variables are the level of specialization of tasks and the level of coordination between team members. These two variables are combined to form the following 2 x 2 matrix.

TYPES OF TEAMS

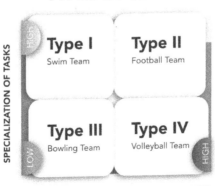

COORDINATION BETWEEN TEAM MEMBERS

Type I—Swim Team: Such teams have a low level of coordination between members, and each team member has a specialised role/task. For example, one team member may specialise in the breaststroke, while another is particularly skilled in the butterfly stroke. Each member will swim their race, relying on their individual skills with little coordination with other teammates.

Type II—Football Team: Whether you're thinking about American football or soccer, those teams feature a high level of co-ordination between players along with highly specialised skills. There are distinct positions/roles team members play. However, all the positions must work together if the team is to succeed.

Type III—Bowling Team: There is a low level of coordination between team members; everyone bowls their individual set. There is also a low level of specialisation of tasks. Each member of the team has the same job—use the bowling ball to knock down the pins.

Type IV—Volleyball Team: In this case, a high level of coordination is required amongst team members. However, there is little specialization of tasks, since team members rotate through the various positions on the court.

Question #5: How will you work together?

This final question helps to make it all very practical. This is where the rubber meets the road—where team members establish the operating norms. Once developed and approved by the team, your norms then become the basis for holding each other accountable.

It's important to establish your norms early in the game—rather than waiting until problems occur and people are stressed to then try to figure out some ground rules or terms of engagement. The following example from my HR high-performance team illustrates this particular lesson.

Our high-performance HR Department's purpose was to foster a culture of learning and development to maximise individual and organisational potential. We also made a commitment to lead by example. This meant we invested significant time and energy in our own learning and development and ensured that it resulted in higher levels of performance. This meant that most team members were actively engaged in some form of professional development.

At a point in time, we identified a performance gap throughout the organisation that required training in managerial accounting. The employees targeted for the training intervention were somewhat less than enthusiastic since the subject matter was considered difficult and required passing a final exam. I instructed Brendalie, my assistant manager, to enrol in the course along with the identified employees.

I didn't exactly consult with Brendalie when making that decision. As a result, I did not take into consideration that she was already pursuing other studies. Because of the trust that existed within our team, Brendalie was comfortable enough to tell me that she found my "request" somewhat unreasonable. I referenced our commitment to learning and development and maximising potential. In doing so, I pointed out that it was my role as her manager to stretch her. Without missing a beat, she responded that a rubber band could be stretched only so much before it broke.

As a result of that experience, as a team we discussed what someone should do when she felt she was being stretched too much. Going forward, it was agreed that any member of the team could request relief simply by saying their rubber band was at its maximum capacity. Because of your strong foundation of trust and genuine caring, no one ever worried that this accommodation would be abused.

Application Exercise:
Create a Team Charter

Schedule time with your team to begin to work on your team charter. Utilise the five questions presented in this chapter to work through the process. Don't just spring this exercise on them. It's important to give them notice and to share with them the reason why you're making this request of them. In articulating your reason, remember to ensure you include a compelling why—something that will motivate and inspire your team members to collaborate with you on this important initiative.

Identifying and Resolving Team Dysfunctions

"Great teams make clear and timely decisions and move forward with complete buy-in from every member of the team, even those who voted against the decision. They leave meetings confident that no one on the team is quietly harbouring doubts about whether to support the actions agreed on."
—Patrick Lencioni[xxv]

The HR team I introduced at the beginning of the chapter was a great team. We made clear and timely decisions. We moved forward with complete buy-in from every member of the team—whether or not they initially supported the idea or plan in question. When we left meetings, we were all confident that all members could be relied upon to actively contribute to the implementation of the decision/plan. That's where we ended up—it wasn't where we started.

To become a great, high-performing team, we had to learn how to overcome some typical team dysfunctions. I attribute a large measure of this accomplishment to Patrick Lencioni and his bestselling book,

JOAN H. UNDERWOOD

The Five Dysfunctions of a Team. In 2004, one of my mentors gifted me that book. When I opened it, I found a Post-it note referring me to page 204. Here's what I found on that page:

Teams that fear conflict…

- Have boring meetings
- Create environments where back-channel politics and personal attacks thrive
- Ignore controversial topics that are critical to team success
- Fail to tap into all the opinions and perspectives of team members
- Waste time and energy with posturing and interpersonal risk management

Teams that engage in conflict…

- Have lively, interesting meetings
- Extract and exploit the ideas of all team members
- Solve real problems quickly
- Minimise politics
- Put critical topics on the table for discussion

Of course, I wanted everything on the second list and none of what was on the first list. So I voraciously devoured every word in that book. Later, as I incorporated Lencioni's model in my training practice, I utilised his field guide to help others pursue the path to success.

As you work to build your own high-performance team, here are some of the obstacles that you will need to navigate along with some proven strategies to help ensure that you are not undone by them.

Absence of Trust

Beginning in Chapter 1 and continuing throughout the book, I have emphasised the importance of trust—both of being trustworthy yourself and of trusting the members of your team. Remember the Law of the Harvest: to reap trust, you first have to sow the seeds of trust. We also unpacked the different components of trust—namely competence, character, benevolence, and consistency. If any of these are missing from your team, the deficit must be resolved if you are to become a high-performance team.

Trust requires vulnerability. With vulnerability comes the risk of being hurt. No one wants to be hurt. As human beings, we are hard-wired for self-preservation. As the team leader, the onus is on you to show that it is safe to be vulnerable. To do so, you must be willing to authentically share and open yourself up to feedback about your weaknesses, mistakes, and fears. It is important to receive feedback from a place of humility and curiosity. If you consistently model that behaviour, the members of your team are likely to follow your lead.

Fear of Conflict

There is nothing inherently bad about conflict. After all, it is nothing more than a difference in opinion or perspective. The danger lies in adopting a dysfunctional approach to handling conflict. The dysfunction may manifest as avoidance or aggression or even violence. With trust at its foundation, your team will not be afraid to engage in constructive conflict. Trust sets the stage for lively and rigorous debates which focus on issues and ideas (as opposed to personalities and motives).

As you embrace your new role as manager, be cautious that you aren't lulled into a false sense of security if your team tends to agree on everything. What you are interpreting as agreement could actually be the manifestation of the fear of conflict. In such cases, you should utilise open-ended questions to invite challenges and the expression of different perspectives, and reassure your team that it is not only safe to disagree, but essential if you are to arrive at the best possible solutions.

Lack of Commitment

Since our goal as managers is to get things done with and through others, commitment is akin to the holy grail. As a manager, I have seen commitment, and I have seen compliance. Based on those experiences, I can assure you that they are as different as chalk and cheese.

When you have a compliant team, they perform based on the power and authority which your position confers on you. They display no vested interest in securing a positive outcome. In extreme cases, such compliance may even be malicious. Malicious compliance is a term used to refer to instances where employees follow the strict letter of the rules even when it is obvious that doing so will lead to unwelcome, unintended consequences.[xxvi] In such instances, it is quite obvious that by exercising some discretion or making a judgment call, the employee in question could secure a more positive outcome.[20]

A simple example of malicious compliance would be an employee submitting expense reports for miniscule claims—e.g. $1.50—to irritate a manager who is considered unreasonable and a stickler for the rules. In such instances, the cost of processing the claim far exceeds the amount being claimed. Further, the amount of the claim is so negligible that the employee derives no meaningful benefit from it being settled.

In contrast, when you have a committed team, the members are ready and willing to perform and see their contributions as part of something bigger than themselves—a higher purpose. Committed employees are engaged. Therefore, they routinely give you the benefit

---

[20] https://www.reddit.com/r/MaliciousCompliance/

of discretionary effort—i.e. they go above and beyond the call of duty to help secure the targeted outcomes.

To secure commitment and not just compliance, you need to leverage trust and facilitate constructive engagement in conflict. When decisions are made in a trusting environment and differing opinions are taken into consideration, you can then call on your team members to commit to pursuing the agreed-upon course of action. That is the framework within which you can avoid or overcome the next obstacle to high performance.

Avoidance of Accountability

One of the hallmarks of a poorly performing team is a lack of accountability. In Chapter 5, I introduced you the Accountability Ladder and encouraged you to operate from the upper rungs. That translates into acknowledging reality and finding and implementing solutions. Patrick Lencioni defines accountability as the willingness of team members to remind one another when they are not living up to the performance standards of the group. In high-performance teams, everyone experiences both intrinsic and extrinsic motivation to contribute their best efforts.

High-performance teams and the people who make up such teams are not perfect. Therefore, there will be times when they miss the mark. What distinguishes them from regular work teams is what happens next. High-performance teams and their members own their mistakes in a way that is devoid of judgment or castigation of the individual and focused on achieving positive change going forward. I'll illustrate this approach by drawing on an incident with my HR team.

The late submission of statutory payroll contributions attracted a financial penalty. One month, as a result of an unanticipated challenge, we were late in preparing the submission and incurred a 10% financial penalty. Clearly, this was not included in our budget. So it had significant adverse implications. When I sat with our personnel officer to discuss the incident, we focused on what had happened and what we could do going forward to ensure there was no recurrence. Due to that incident and the brainstorming that ensued, we updated our standard operating procedures to give ourselves a bigger time cushion for the submission of the contributions.

Inattention to Results

Even the best teams have to safeguard against becoming too complacent and losing focus. It is essential that we find ways to individually and collectively keep our eyes on the prize. Perhaps you've heard the expression: *what gets measured gets done.* In my high-performing HR team, we had a regular schedule of reporting on our individual and departmental performance against objectives.[21] Therefore, we were able to flag concerns early and to take the necessary steps to get back on track.

As you seek to have your team develop a results-oriented mindset, it is important to be on the lookout for hidden or conflicting agendas. In high-performance teams, the departmental objectives supersede personal agendas. With that understanding, team members are willing to assist a colleague if she requires such assistance to meet a departmental goal. That type of support is readily forthcoming, because team members know that they can expect their colleagues to reciprocate if and when the need arises.

Caveat

Before we move on, I have one final word of caution. The interpersonal bonds between members of a high-performance team can

---

[21] I'll share more about this when we discuss great meetings in Chapter 17.

become very strong. My team members and I have genuine love and affection for one another. In such cases, it is possible that the needs of individual members and the relationships could take precedence over the organisational imperatives.

As the leader, it is important that you set the tone—making it clear that it is not a choice between relationship and task, but rather a case of taking care of both the task and the shared relationships.

Yet another pitfall is the possibility of workers forming cliques. The bonds that exist in a clique differ in nature and motive from those which characterise the relationships in a high-performance team. Cliques are often born out of a sense of superiority. The members take pleasure in excluding others and in somehow making those outside the clique feel less than… In contrast, high-performance team members often form genuine bonds of affection. However, the ties that bind them together do not serve the dual purpose of restricting them from developing healthy relationships with other individuals who are not members of the team.

Therefore, if you decide to work towards creating a high-performance team, both you and your direct reports should exercise due care and caution to ensure you do not lose focus on the team's purpose and the associated goals, and that you do not deteriorate into a clique.

 Application Exercise: Identify and Resolve Your Team Dysfunctions

1. Revisit Lencioni's 5 Team Dysfunctions Model.
2. Where do you think your team stands in relation to these five dysfunctions?

3. What are some specific actions you could take to begin to overcome the dysfunctions which might currently exist on your team?

4. What is one thing that you are prepared to do within the next 72 hours to begin to resolve those problems?

5. On a scale of 1 to 10, with 10 being completely and totally committed, how committed are you to taking that action?

Team Roles and Responsibilities

"The basic building block of good teambuilding is for a leader to promote the feeling that ev'ery human being is unique and adds value."
—Anonymous

Throughout Part II of this book, I repeatedly emphasised the importance of taking the time to understand the people you lead. In this chapter, as we wrap up our examination of high-performance teams, we will turn our attention to how you can bring all that knowledge and understanding together to optimise the performance of each member of your team. In doing so, you ultimately maximise overall team performance.

As the team leader, it is your responsibility to get to know each of your direct reports and how they tend to show up. You can then leverage that insight when assigning team roles and responsibilities. If we turn to basketball for an analogy, the team coach or captain needs to know the strengths of each player and to capitalise on them in designing the game strategy. For example, if you have a player who is strong on the defensive boards but is not a very good ball handler, you accommodate those realities by ensuring he can pass the ball to a teammate who can then move it up the court and set the stage for a strong offensive play.

Familiarity with the individual strengths and weaknesses and likes and dislikes of the members of my high-performing HR team enabled me to craft a similar game plan. Blanka had great aptitude—and an inexplicable liking—for running payroll. While the rest of the team dreaded the repetitive nature of the data entry and the minutiae of making all the adjustments for the various types of leave, overtime, and other non-routine entries, she actually took pleasure in completing each payroll. She challenged herself to complete each payroll run ahead of schedule and error free. Because of my awareness of her preferences, and the dislikes of the other members of the team, I devised a strategy which was eagerly embraced by all. Blanka became our payroll guru, and I designated two other team members to cover when she was on leave or otherwise unavailable. However, even in her absence, we still thought of it as Blanka's payroll.

Belbin's Team Roles

Over the years, I've experimented with several models in my quest to gain the insights necessary for me to better understand and lead my teams. There is one particular model I embraced early in my leadership journey and which continues to serve me well today. The model in question is Belbin's Team[22] Roles.

Belbin *et al* have identified nine team roles along with the contributions such individuals typically make in a team context. And because none of us are perfect, the team roles also include a list of allowable weaknesses. With the kind permission of BELBIN Associates,

---

[22] Dr. Meredith Belbin and his team discovered there are nine clusters of behaviour—these were called 'Belbin Team Roles'. For further information, please visit https://www.belbin.com/about/belbin-team-roles/.

JOAN H. UNDERWOOD

I've reproduced the team role summaries for your information and understanding.

Belbin® Team Role Summary Descriptions

 Resource Investigator

Contribution: Outgoing, enthusiastic. Explores opportunities and develops contacts.

Allowable Weaknesses: Might be over-optimistic, and can lose interest once the initial enthusiasm has passed.

 Teamworker

Contribution: Co-operative, perceptive and diplomatic. Listens and averts friction.

Allowable Weaknesses: Can be indecisive in crunch situations and tends to avoid confrontation.

 Co-ordinator

Contribution: Mature, confident, identifies talent. Clarifies goals. Delegates effectively.

Allowable Weaknesses: Can be seen as manipulative and might offload their own share of the work.

 Plant

Contribution: Creative, imaginative, free-thinking. Generates ideas and solves difficult problems.

Allowable Weaknesses: Might ignore incidentals, and may be too pre-occupied to communicate effectively.

 Monitor Evaluator

Contribution: Sober, strategic and discerning. Sees all options and judges accurately.

Allowable Weaknesses: Sometimes lacks the drive and ability to inspire others and can be overly critical.

 Specialist

Contribution: Single-minded, self-starting and dedicated. They provide specialist knowledge and skills.

Allowable Weaknesses: Can only contribute on a narrow front and tends to dwell on the technicalities.

 Shaper

Contribution: Challenging, dynamic, thrives on pressure. Has the drive and courage to overcome obstacles.

Allowable Weaknesses: Can be prone to provocation, and may sometimes offend people's feelings.

 Implementer

Contribution: Practical, reliable, efficient. Turns ideas into actions and organises work that needs to be done.

Allowable Weaknesses: Can be a bit inflexible and slow to respond to new possibilities.

 Completer Finisher

Contribution: Painstaking, conscientious, anxious. Searches out errors. Polishes and perfects.

Allowable Weaknesses: Can be inclined to worry unduly, and reluctant to delegate.

For more information:
+44 (0)1223 264975 | www.belbin.com

© BELBIN® 2016. 'BELBIN' is a registered trademark of BELBIN ASSOCIATES, UK.

BELBIN

Can a Person Change Team Roles?

Perhaps as you read the role descriptions, one or more of them resonates with you in terms of how you tend to show up in a team. Or perhaps you recognise some of your colleagues or direct reports. It is important to understand that the team roles provide information about an individual's default or preferred behaviours. However, as we established in Chapter 1 when we discussed emotional intelligence, self-awareness paves the way for self-regulation. Therefore, once you realise that you are predisposed to behave in a certain way, you can analyse the situation to ascertain if that behaviour is what the team requires at that particular point in time.

As you lead your team, please bear in mind that an individual's team roles may develop and mature. They may change with experience and conscious attention. Different team roles may also come to the fore in response to the needs of particular situations.

Team Role Sacrifice

In some circumstances, an individual will need to forego using their preferred team role and adopt another in its place. This shift may be rendered necessary due to the lack of a desired role in the team or because another person is already fulfilling the preferred team role. For example, I recently facilitated a teambuilding programme for the management team of one of my corporate clients. Several members of the executive team showed up as Shapers. However, the team lacked Monitor Evaluators.

As illustrated in the team role summary descriptions, Shapers tend to be dynamic, thrive on pressure, and have the drive to overcome obstacles. Those are very important leadership traits. However, it is equally important for the team to be strategic and discerning and to see all options and judge them accurately. That type of contribution

JOAN H. UNDERWOOD

typically comes from a Monitor Evaluator. Since no one on the team was naturally inclined to fulfil that role, a decision would need to be taken about who was best positioned to be designated as the Monitor Evaluator for a particular project. That individual would then be called upon to make a team role sacrifice in the best interests of the team.

As the team leader, it is important for you to have a sense of each member's preferred role(s). You also need to be mindful of what the team needs at any given point in time so that you can appropriately deploy the resources that are available to you—up to and including requesting that people make a team role sacrifice in the best interests of attaining high-performance status.

Caveat

When it comes to team role sacrifices, I have two words of caution. Firstly, it would be prudent to be very mindful of an individual's allowable weaknesses when requesting that they take on a team role sacrifice. For example, one of Resource Investigators' allowable weaknesses is that they can lose interest once the initial enthusiasm for a project has passed. Given that fact, you might want to think twice before asking such an individual to take on the role of a Completer Finisher, whose primary contribution to the team is to be painstaking and conscientious, searching out errors, and polishing and perfecting the output.

Secondly, don't lose sight of the word sacrifice in the name. Asking someone to assume a role that is not the preferred or default is truly a sacrifice. So you are cautioned to be judicious in making the request. Specifically, acknowledge that it is, in fact, a sacrifice—and be careful that you don't deplete goodwill by making the request too frequently, and without appropriately expressing appreciation when the individual takes one for the team.

Personal Reflection Exercise: Determine Your Preferred Team Role

1. I invite you to devote some time to reflecting on how you have shown up on teams in the past.
2. Which of the nine Belbin Team Roles seem most evident in your past behaviour?
3. Which team role resonates the least with you?
4. How might you build capacity in that area—just in case you need to make a team role sacrifice?

As a special bonus for having purchased this book, you are now entitled to a 40% discount on your personal Belbin Team Role report. To access this discount, please visit https://www.belbin.com/belbin-for-individuals/ and utilise the code **UTDS40JK** to access your Managers' First Aid Kit discount. Please note that this discounted price of US $42 is restricted to readers of this book.

CHAPTER SIXTEEN

COACHING FOR PERFORMANCE

Each person holds so much power within themselves that needs to be let out. Sometimes they just need a little nudge, a little direction, a little support, a little coaching, and the greatest things can happen.

–Pete Carroll[xxvii]

What's in it for You?

AS I'VE STATED IN PREVIOUS CHAPTERS, YOUR ROLE AS A LEADER IS to get things done with and through others. To unleash the talent that resides within your team, you must be able to coach your direct reports. Don't just take my word for it. The International Coaching Federation (ICF) conducted a global study[23] which found *inter alia* that:

- Coaching brings a shift in corporate culture that increases productivity by changing it from command and control to collaboration and creativity.

---

[23] 2016 ICF Global Coaching Study

- Individual clients reported a median return on investment of 3.44 times their investment.
- Companies that use or have used professional coaching for business reasons have a median return on investment of seven times their initial investment.

Now, just in case you're worried that you have to become a professional coach on top of everything else, let me hasten to point out that what I'm advocating is that you utilise coaching skills and approaches to manage your team and help maximise individual performance. This is separate and distinct from being a trained professional coach.

Of course, if you're absolutely certain that you and your team have already realised your full potential, then you need read no further. However, if you're anything like the rest of us, and you're looking for a way to take your performance to the next level, then coaching just might be the key to unlock that door.

In this chapter, we begin by looking at the four primary needs that business coaching is designed to meet. We then turn our attention to building the coaching relationship. We conclude by sharing key strategies for conducting successful coaching sessions.

Four Primary Needs Met by Coaching

As with so many other things in life, it is helpful to begin with the end in mind. In other words, to ensure that the coaching provided is fit for purpose, we need to have clarity on the precise nature of the need we're seeking to meet. But before we get into that, let's clarify what we mean by coaching.

The ICF defines coaching as "partnering with clients in a thought-provoking and creative process that inspires them to maximise their personal and professional potential even in the face of growing complexity and uncertainty, which is common in many workplaces today that are struggling with the war for talent."[24]

In addition to the proffered definition of coaching, it is important for all parties to understand what coaching isn't—

- Coaching is not the same as consulting, where someone is hired/brought in because of their specific expertise to recommend solutions to problems experienced by the company/client.
- Coaching is definitely not counselling. The latter is focused primarily on examining and understanding the past. In contrast, coaching is oriented towards the future.
- Coaching is not mentoring. Mentors draw on their own experiences to offer guidance and direction to clients.
- Coaching is not training. Effective training creates a curriculum based on pre-determined learning objectives. In contrast, objectives in a coaching relationship are personalised based on the specific needs of the coachee.

So, having established both what coaching is and what it isn't, let's now examine the different objectives managers can satisfy in coaching their direct reports.

1. Coaching for Skills Acquisition

Employees who find themselves in a new role may be less than optimally equipped to meet performance expectations. As a result, they may make repeated mistakes, miss deadlines, fail to meet targets or performance standards, etc.

A classic example is that of a new supervisor or manager who reverts to doing the work of the line staff when the departmental

---

[24] https://bit.ly/3lXlOuo

workload peaks. As a result, the duties related to planning, leading, organising, and controlling the workflow are neglected. (Remember Lydia from the Introduction?) The likelihood of this occurring is indirectly proportional to the individual's comfort level/proficiency in the various supervisory or managerial competencies—i.e. the more comfortable you are in your new role as a manager, the less likely you are to revert to executing line staff duties when the going gets tough.

It is somewhat paradoxical that a new manager who jumps in and executes line staff duties when things get busy probably views their actions as tangible evidence of a strong commitment to securing the success of the organisation. Years ago, I had one client—a senior engineer with a telecoms company—proudly describe an incident where he rolled up his sleeves and dug the trench to run a cable. He went on to complain that his executive manager had not expressed any appreciation for his having taken that initiative.

Part of the irony of that situation is that the senior engineer's executive manager had described that same incident to me. However, he used it to illustrate the point that the individual did not understand his role within the organisation. For the executive manager, it wasn't a matter of commitment, but rather a case of inefficiency.

As I debriefed the incident with the engineer, I invited him to consider what it cost the company to have someone at his level spend time on a task that could have been done by an entry-level employee. The concept of opportunity cost was not something he had taken into consideration…

2. Coaching for Performance Improvement

This may be the circumstance when the need for coaching is most evident from an organisational perspective. An employee who might have a good track record may have registered a sudden or more

JOAN H. UNDERWOOD

gradual decline and is now at the point where concerns have arisen. Based on past performance, it's not likely that the suboptimal performance is due to a lack of skills. In the context of a coaching relationship, the precise nature of the performance gap can be identified and may be traced to factors such as a loss of motivation, challenges with work-life balance, interpersonal dynamics, etc.

In any event, an effective coach can engage the employee to ascertain the factors contributing to a decline in performance. Together, they can then identify strategies for addressing the problem and getting the coachee back to the traditional high-functioning state.

3. Coaching for Career Development

Is there someone on your team who invariably completes work assignments ahead of time and who may be perceived by their peers as something of an overachiever? What about that person who always seems to have time on their hands? While it may seem counterintuitive, this person is a great candidate for coaching. Instead of thinking that they are fine and one less thing for you to worry about, you should see it as an opportunity for you to help them level up. The focus in that instance would not be on improving performance, but rather on jointly identifying opportunities for stretch assignments which would serve both to challenge and acknowledge the valuable contribution they make to the team.

Such coaching could also be a precursor to a promotion or new assignment or participation in the organisation's succession planning programme. Alternatively, it may simply serve to maintain or improve motivation for those employees who thrive on self-actualization—i.e. setting and accomplishing new goals.

4. Coaching for Change

In this context, the change could be either individual or organisational. What is important is that the individual experiences difficulty in adapting to the new circumstances and that difficulty results in a performance gap. In such a situation, the role of the coach is to help the coachee navigate the change and to develop and implement strategies for excelling in the new normal.

 ## Application Exercise: Identify Your Direct Reports' Coaching Needs

Before we move on, please take a moment to think about how you can apply the lessons contained in this section to help your staff.

1. Make a list of all your direct reports.
2. Next to each name, write down the type of coaching you think would be most helpful to that employee.
3. Keep that information safe. We will return to it later in the chapter.

Building the Coaching Relationship

A good relationship starts with good communication.

In Chapter 9, we learnt that effective communication is one of the six fundamental building blocks of any good relationship. The coaching relationship is no exception. Strong relationships are pivotal to successful coaching. By following these three steps, you can be well on your way to securing strong and mutually beneficial coaching relationships with your direct reports.

Establish Rapport

Rapport is a state of mutual trust. Trust can be hard to establish and easy to lose. In a June 2014 article, HR.com recommended the following five tips for building and maintaining rapport:

1. **Be curious**: Ask lots of questions. In addition to enabling you to glean valuable information, your skilful use of questions sends a clear message that you are interested in the individual. *(By the way, how are you coming along with that Building an Essential Habit exercise from Chapter 3?)*

2. **Listen attentively**: In the absence of attentive listening, your skilful use of questions goes to waste. Your attentive listening will yield dividends in that you will gain both information and better understanding of the individual. Such understanding then paves the way for empathy, which is yet another one of the essential relationship building blocks.

3. **Utilise mirroring**: The study of neurolinguistics has shown that we can establish subconscious bonds when we mirror the demeanour, language, and breathing patterns of the people with whom we engage. Don't worry. At this stage it's not necessary (yet) for you to become a Jedi Master. It will suffice for you to be attentive and to use body language which signifies that you are open and engaged.

4. **Focus intently**: The coachee should be the centre of attention during your interactions. Eliminate all distractions and let the coachee know that you have done so. If you give in to the temptation to multitask, you risk creating the impression that you are not committed to supporting your direct reports, and that you do not think they are as important as whatever else is distracting you.

5. **Display understanding**: Having applied the preceding tips, it is then important to reinforce the bond by showing that you understand and can relate to what the coachee has shared. The caveat here is that showing understanding is not the same as endorsing/agreeing with what has been shared. Rather, it is about acknowledging that you have truly heard and appreciated what has been shared.

Define Relationship and Terms of Engagement

To maximise the value of a coaching relationship, it is essential to ensure that parties understand the precise nature of the relationship and that expectations are managed. From the outset, the coach and coachee need to establish the specific terms of engagement. Here again it is useful to make certain key distinctions.

Coaching is about providing guidance as opposed to issuing commands and directives. A metaphor I have found to be particularly helpful in reminding me to stay in coach position is that of a guide on the side instead of a sage on the stage.

Coaching is about providing support as opposed to issuing rewards and punishment. Clearly, as a manager, issuing rewards and punishments falls under your purview. However, you should keep any such discussions separate and distinct from your coaching conversations so that your employees continue to view the coaching space as totally supportive and developmental.

Coaches facilitate development and growth as opposed to mandating compliance. Compliance is generally associated with a big stick or command-and-control mentality. In contrast, coaching conversations are collaborative and create space for the employee to take the lead on identifying solutions.

Coaches have a responsibility to challenge thinking as opposed

JOAN H. UNDERWOOD

to dictating right and wrong. The last thing you should want as a manager is for your team to depend on you to make each and every decision. Rather, you want the members of your team to be optimally empowered and informed. In that way, they will be more likely to utilise their best judgment to make their decisions and take actions. You can help them hone those skills during your coaching conversations. In step 1, we emphasised the importance of skilful questioning. Your skilful questions will serve to challenge your direct reports' thinking and help them to gain greater insight, which then leads to better decision making.

Maintain the Relationship

Once established, you must carefully nurture the coaching relationship. The following tips can help to realise that objective:

- Allow the coachee to act autonomously. Remember that your role is to get things done with and through others. So let them do it!
- Encourage the coachee to take responsibility. If necessary, you can revisit Chapter 5 to reaffirm the difference between responsibility, accountability, and blame. The bottom line is that you utilise coaching to support your direct reports in identifying an appropriate action plan. They then assume responsibility for implementing the plan, understanding fully that you will hold them accountable for fulfilling the commitments they made.
- Support the learning and development process by reviewing accomplishments and setting new goals. Coaching is ongoing—it's not a once-and-done arrangement. The best way for you to support your direct reports is to be guided by the West African tradition of Sankofa, which posits that the

past illuminates the present. Sankofa[25] teaches us that we should reach back and gather the best of what our past has to teach us, so that we can achieve our full potential as we move forward.

• Once you have established a solid platform in a coaching relationship, attention can then turn to addressing the performance of the coachee.

GROWing Your Staff

The GROW Model has been seen to yield higher productivity, improved communication, better interpersonal relationships, and a better quality working environment.
–Performance Consultants[26]

My go-to tool for performance coaching is the GROW Model created by Sir John Whitmore[xxviii] and colleagues. Although there is no single right way to coach, in my experience (which includes coaching as well as training managers to coach) I have found the GROW Model easy to understand and apply, and quick to produce results. At the beginning of my two-day performance coaching workshop, I typically tell participants that by the end of day 2, they would have coached and been coached by a peer, and that in each instance the coachee would have created a plan of action to resolve a real problem. At that point, participants tend to be somewhat incredulous. However, they invariably come around.

I remember a particular workshop participant who was respectful yet adamant as she advised me she would only be attending the first day, since she had other work obligations and could not afford

[25] https://www.berea.edu/cgwc/the-power-of-sankofa/

[26] http://www.performanceconsultants.com/grow-model

to spend two days away from her desk. Based on our conversation, I was quite surprised when she walked into the training room on day 2 of the workshop. When I expressed my surprise, she enthusiastically assured me that based on how much she learnt the day before, and how relevant it was to her work, she was not prepared to miss out on day 2.

That appreciation for performance coaching and its potential positive impact on managerial efficacy has been almost universal among other workshop participants, as evidenced in the following excerpts from the workshop evaluation forms:

> *"Performance coaching leads to self-discovery and productivity."*
> *"This is game changing."*
> *"All managers should coach."*
> *"I am ready to advocate for performance coaching in my workplace."*
> *"I can do this!"*

So, let me introduce you to the GROW Model, so that you can determine for yourself whether you agree with me and the thousands—if not millions—of managers worldwide who have enthusiastically embraced this system of performance coaching.

The name itself is an acronym depicting the elements of the four-part model. As indicated in the following diagramme, the first step is to identify the goal—i.e. what is to be accomplished. The next step is to describe the current reality—i.e. the level of performance relative to the stated goal. That is then followed by the identification of options that the employee could pursue to close the gap between the goal and the current reality. In the final step, you secure a commitment by having the employee assert what they will do going forward. Let's take a deeper dive into each of the four steps in the process.

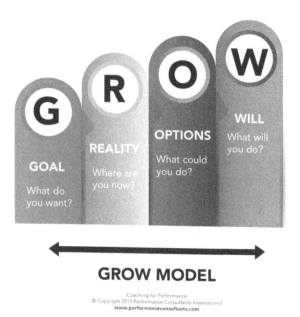

GROW MODEL

Coaching for Performance
© Copyright 2014 Performance Consultants International
www.performanceconsultants.com

Goal

As I mentioned before, if you don't know where you're going, any road can get you there. Well, perhaps that sentiment informed the decision on how to start this tried and proven approach to structuring a coaching conversation. It is absolutely essential to devote the necessary time and energy to collaboratively identify and agree on the desired results—both the specific coaching conversation and the broader coaching relationship.

As the manager, you need to lead this discussion. In the context of a performance coaching conversation, both parties should reach consensus on the goal, since it will form the basis for assessing the level of progress and, ultimately, success. It is also important to ensure that the goal aligns with the broader departmental/organisational objectives. When you begin with the end in mind and clarify expectations, it significantly reduces the likelihood of unexpected surprises further down the road.

JOAN H. UNDERWOOD

Reality

In this second stage of the process, you and your direct report discuss and agree on what currently obtains—i.e. you identify and discuss the status quo. In the case of a performance assessment, the discussion would cover how the employee is currently performing relative to established standards. In addition to examining the status quo vis-a-vis performance, this is also the time when you should explore issues such as the employee's beliefs about the job and their performance, along with any concerns, challenges, or constraints they're experiencing.

Opportunity

Having established the goal and ascertained the current realities, the next step in the process is to identify possible options for moving forward. This can be compared to a brainstorming phase, where you and your direct report identify the various avenues for moving forward in pursuit of the goal established in the first step of the process.

Ensure that you make this phase as expansive and exhaustive as possible—exploring the pros and cons of the various courses of action along with decision criteria for making the final selection. It is absolutely essential that both you and your direct report continually refer to the goal established in Step 1 in order to secure alignment.

Yet another variable that you should include in this step of the process is a candid discussion about the employee's feelings regarding the various options. This is geared towards safeguarding the selection of an opportunity which is completely unpalatable to the employee.

Will/Way Forward

In this final stage of the process, you must secure a firm commitment on the way forward. The output from this stage is a plan of action, including the identification of possible obstacles as well as risk mitigation factors, and an agreement on the process for follow-up, monitoring, and evaluation. Key to the process as well is a clear understanding and assignment of responsibilities along with associated timelines.

I strongly encourage you to check for the coachee's level of commitment to the plan of action prior to concluding the coaching conversation. One way this can be done is by inviting employees to use a rating scale to articulate their level of commitment. My typical question is, "On a scale of 1 to 10, with 10 being totally committed, how would you rate your level of commitment to this plan of action?"

Personally, I like to follow up the response by asking, "Is that level of commitment sufficient for you to take action on this?" If they say yes, then I proceed to schedule a date and time for our follow-up session. If they say no, then I open up the conversation by asking what it would take for them to be sufficiently motivated to do something about closing the performance gap. At times, that question leads to further brainstorming and the identification of a plan of action to which the employee is more committed.

Additional Considerations

There are a few final pointers I would like to share to assist you in effectively utilizing the GROW Model. A coach's toolkit is simply incomplete without the following three skills.

1. Skilful use of powerful questions—I know I mentioned the importance of skilful questions before, but it's definitely

worth repeating! The most powerful questions are open-ended, generative, and non-judgmental.

- Open-ended questions are those that cannot be answered by a simple yes or no.
- Generative questions are those which come from a place of curiosity and are designed to explore possibilities.
- Non-judgmental questions reject the notion of being critical of the individual. Even if you don't understand the reasoning, you're encouraged to be curious—as opposed to critical—about the employee's thought process.

2. Active listening—listening to understand and not just to answer or challenge; listening from a place of curiosity; listening not just with ears but with eyes and heart to discover underlying meaning and intent; and

3. Flexibility—while we have presented the model in a linear manner, it is important to note that the process may need to be iterative to derive optimal benefit.

For additional information on the GROW Model, including sample questions you can utilise in your coaching conversations, you can visit http://www.performanceconsultants.com/grow-model.

 Application Exercise: Conduct a Performance Coaching Conversation

Please return to the list you made during the exercise at the end of the first section in this chapter.

1. Select one of your direct reports from the list.
2. Revisit the type of coaching conversation you indicated you should have with that employee. Has anything shifted for

you now that you've completed the chapter? If so, what type of coaching conversation do you now think you should have with that individual?

3. What do you think should be your goal for that coaching conversation?

4. Once you have identified the goal for the conversation, go ahead and schedule it. Please ensure you choose a mutually convenient time and that you let them know the agenda for the meeting.

5. Prepare for the coaching conversation by visiting http:// www.performanceconsultants.com/grow-model and creating a list of questions to help guide you through the coaching conversation.

6. Document the decisions taken and set a date for a follow-up conversation.

7. After the coaching conversation, spend some time reflecting on what worked well and what you can do to make the next conversation even better.

CHAPTER SEVENTEEN

CONDUCTING GREAT MEETINGS

*"A meeting is an event at which the minutes
are kept, and the hours are lost."*

–Anonymous

End the Hostage Crisis

I F YOU'VE NEVER FELT LIKE YOU WERE BEING HELD HOSTAGE IN A series of never-ending, non-productive meetings, then you can probably skip this chapter. However, if you're like the thousands and thousands (if not millions and millions) of us who are frustrated by frequent meetings plagued by a lack of clear purpose, no meaningful conclusions, failure to follow up, and a myriad of other ills, then read on. A measure of relief just might be in sight.

My biggest peeve about meetings is a lack of clarity about the purpose. I find it so frustrating when I receive a meeting invitation and the only information included is the date, time, and place. Without knowing what the meeting is about, I'm constrained in my ability to prepare so that I can make a meaningful contribution. Perhaps you have the enviable gift of being able to come up with brilliant strategies complete with pros and cons and risk and cost/benefit analysis of said strategy on the spur of the moment… If so, great! For the rest of us, some advance notice is required, unless the only reason for inviting us is to make up the numbers.

My second biggest peeve is meetings which end without any clear decisions or accountability for the decisions that might have been taken. Oh, and to exacerbate the already bad situation, no summary is provided in the wake of the meeting. Such meetings invariably lead to inaction and a lack of follow-up or follow-through. As the Chinese proverb wisely points out, "The palest ink is better than the best memory." If that one doesn't work for you, you should also note that, "The mind is a terrible place to store important information."

So, in your role as manager, I strongly encourage you to take note of the following tips designed to help you as well as the hapless folks whom you may have unwittingly been holding hostage up to this point in time:

1. Always distribute an agenda. An agenda including the purpose of the meeting should be distributed to all participants well in advance of the meeting.
2. Ensure you have the right people in the room. Large meetings with attendees who are disengaged encourage social loafing, while the failure to have the right people in the room can prevent you from making decisions or from having the information you need to make the best possible decisions.
3. Keep the meeting as short as possible. The optimal duration will depend on the nature of the meeting (e.g. brainstorming, decision-making, planning, etc.). Bear in mind that work expands to fill the space available. If participants know that only an hour has been allocated for the meeting, they are less likely to squander the time.

JOAN H. UNDERWOOD

4. Send out meeting notes. The sooner you do this, the better. Sending out a summary of salient points, decisions taken, action items, due dates, and people responsible for said action items helps to create and/or maintain a sense of urgency—especially if you do so within twenty-four hours of the meeting.

5. Follow up. This is yet another way you can communicate and reinforce the importance of the subject matter. Folks are busy, so if you don't follow up, your issues are likely to be placed on the back burner (or may fall off the stove completely!).

If you follow those five tips, much fewer people are likely to feel like you're holding them hostage. However, what if you're not the meeting convener but one of the hostages? Well, there's light at the end of the tunnel for you as well. In *Secrets to Masterful Meetings*, Michael Wilkinson[xxix] dedicates a chapter to those of us who want to take action to break free rather than continue to suffer in silence. Here are a few of his tips for politely breaking a hostage impasse:

Meeting doesn't have a purpose or agenda: In such cases, you need to respectfully but firmly exert some influence to get the meeting back on track—or to find it a track if it never had one. Here's an example of some appropriate language as proposed by Wilkinson to accomplish that goal:

"Excuse me. I may have missed it. Could you take a second to go over the overall purpose of this meeting, what we need to have when we are done, and your thoughts about the agenda? This will help me stay focused and make sure I don't go off on tangents."

The discussion is getting off track: The appropriate strategy here is to acknowledge and commend the good work that has already been accomplished and gently but firmly steer the conversation back to the main topic. In doing so, it may also be useful to inquire whether participants want to put the other topic(s) on the agenda of a subsequent meeting.

Decisions or actions are not being documented: Your actions in such cases will depend on whether there is a designated notetaker. If there is, you could ask if they would read back the decision so that everyone is clear going forward. If there is no designated notetaker, then you can suggest that the role is assigned to someone. If you do, be prepared to have the responsibility assigned to you.

The meeting is about to end without a review/summary of decisions: In such an instance, you need to jump into the fray before people start walking out the door (or clicking on the Leave Meeting button). By this time, folks are probably eager to get out the door or to start the meeting after the meeting (I'm sure you know what I mean). Therefore, to get their attention and their support for your recommendation, you need to broach the matter in a way that addresses their self-interest. Here's Wilkinson's suggestion on how you can accomplish that:

"After such a productive meeting, I would hate to leave without being clear on what we decided or what is going to happen next. Could we take a minute to review the decisions we've made and the actions that need to occur once we leave?"

So, whether you're guilty of unintentionally holding others hostage, or whether you're desperately hoping someone will rescue you from the plethora of non-productive meetings, you can utilise the information provided in this chapter to help you replace your personal hostage crisis with a great meeting.

Six Essential Elements for a Great Meeting

So, what exactly constitutes a great meeting? Based on my experience over the years—both as a hostage and as an unwitting hostage taker—I've identified six essential elements for a great meeting:

1. **A clear purpose which is also fit for purpose**—i.e. a meeting is the best-suited medium to accomplish the task at hand
2. **The right people in the "room"**—i.e. the people with the required knowledge, skills, information, and authority
3. **Adequate notice**—timely communication, including the meeting date and time, venue, duration, required preparation, and targeted outcomes
4. **Effective facilitation**—The person chairing the meeting needs to adopt the 5 P's motto, i.e. Proper Preparation Prevents Poor Performance
5. **Timely and aligned action**—this element addresses both the when and how (i.e. quality/standards) associated with the implementation of decisions taken during the meeting
6. **Follow-up and evaluation**—it is absolutely essential to close the loop by reviewing progress to ascertain and ensure that the purpose which was established has, in fact, been met

Having established our working definition for a great meeting, let's now take a deeper dive by applying our minds to what needs to take place before, during, and after said meeting.

> *"The right task + the right people + the right*
> *setting = unprecedented actions."*
> —Marvin Weisbord, adapted by Claros Group

The task of convening a great meeting begins well in advance of the scheduled date and time of the meeting. Let's explore what you need to accomplish before convening the meeting.

Establish a Clear Purpose

So why did you decide to convene a meeting in the first place? Perhaps you have information to share. If that's your primary objective, there may be more effective and efficient ways to disseminate that information. Perhaps you could circulate a report or send an email. If the communication channel you need is one-directional, then a meeting really isn't your best choice/forum. The caveat here is that it's important to ensure you identify a mechanism for people to seek clarification if necessary.

Or perhaps, instead of sharing information, you need input from members of your team or external stakeholders. That is indeed a legitimate purpose for a meeting. However, it is essential that you clearly communicate that to the invitees. Otherwise folks could show up to the meeting without the critical information you need.

In the event that you've determined the purpose of your meeting is to gather information, the next step is to decide exactly how you will accomplish that. Two options include brainstorming and open discussions. You should inform participants of the format of the meeting so they can adequately prepare to contribute.

Sometimes, the purpose for the meeting goes beyond seeking input and holding discussions/brainstorming to actually making decisions. If so, all parties need to be clear on the rules of decision-making. Some of the more popular options include voting or consensus. However, there are times when decisions taken during the meeting might be subject to confirmation or veto by someone higher up in the organisation. Establishing such issues up front can minimise the risk of misunderstandings and dysfunctional conflict.

The bottom line is that, in determining the purpose of your meeting, you can designate it as one of the following six categories:

Status Update Meetings: this category covers your regular team meetings as well as project meetings. These meetings can easily become long and drawn out as participants drone on about what they have been doing. Years ago, I developed a version of the status update meeting that enabled me and my team to secure alignment, preserve a sense of urgency, and eliminate busy, non-productive work. Here's how it worked:

Every morning, we would gather in the common area of our department and take turns answering the following questions. We made it a standing-up meeting to convey a sense of urgency.

1. What's on your plate (agenda) for today?
2. How does that link in/align with the department's strategic objectives?
3. What assistance/support do you require to achieve your goals?

Depending on each person's responses to these questions, we might take a decision to request that people defer their planned agenda in order to pitch in and assist a colleague with a more pressing task.

In addition to helping us remain productive and focused, the meetings—which we dubbed huddles—ensured we were all aware of what was happening. This amped up our department's efficiency as it enabled us to pinch-hit for each other. It also built camaraderie, as people with slim agendas readily volunteered to help out their peers, knowing that their colleagues would reciprocate when the shoe was on the other foot.

Information-Sharing Meetings: As previously mentioned, if your primary goal is to share information, please ask yourself whether a meeting is the most appropriate mechanism to do so, or whether you could disseminate the information via email, memo, a report, etc. If you determine that a meeting really is your best option, I advise that you find ways to engage the participants. Otherwise, you run the risk of them feeling like hostages.

As the convener of an information-sharing meeting, you should note that people process information in different ways and at different speeds. To accommodate those differences, I recommend that—if practicable—you provide the information in multiple formats, e.g. verbally, visually (e.g. PowerPoint), and in writing.

You should allocate time to field questions during the meeting and provide an avenue for people to submit questions, comments, and requests for clarification after the meeting. This feedback loop is important to help ensure you achieve common understanding of the information you shared.

Decision-Making Meetings: If the primary purpose of the meeting is to make a decision, you should communicate this to attendees along with the decision-making process that you intend to use.

Although you would have included information about the decision-making process in the meeting notice, it is prudent to reiterate the process at the beginning of the meeting and confirm participants' understanding of the process before proceeding. This is a safeguard against people objecting to the process if it doesn't yield the result they wanted.

JOAN H. UNDERWOOD

Problem-Solving Meetings: These meetings can be very complex, and it's essential you have optimal involvement from all participants in order to identify the best solutions. The pre-meeting communication is, therefore, very important to ensure participants show up ready, willing, and able to contribute to the discussions.

My principal word of advice for when you're chairing such meetings is to reserve your input until you have heard from the other participants. Otherwise, you run the risk that they will self-censor rather than openly disagree with something you have said.

Secondly, you should establish the solution criteria before you begin the problem solving. By this I mean that participants should agree on what would constitute success. The reason for establishing this before coming up with possible solutions is that you don't want to fall prey to the temptation to reverse-engineer the criteria to fit a solution which seems to be popular.

Finally, when you think you've completed the process, step back and ask everyone to apply their minds to one final question: "What have we overlooked?" or "What's missing?" Keep repeating that question until you have exhausted all the answers.

Innovation/Brainstorming Meetings: When you need to tap into your team's creativity to come up with new ideas, strategies, products, etc., this is the type of meeting you need. Brainstorming meetings require the active engagement and input of all participants. So this is something you need to establish from the get go. That heads-up is particularly important if the culture within your team/organisation tends to be hierarchical or highly bureaucratic, since those factors have a tendency to limit the type of sharing that's required in a brainstorming meeting.

There are lots of resources out there to help you come up with creative ways of facilitating brainstorming. Get adventurous and experiment. Let your creativity flow and remember to assign someone to capture all the wonderful ideas that you and your team will generate.

Team-Building Meetings: Even the best performing teams need to carve out time to work on enhancing their group dynamics. If you're married, it might help to think of it as comparable to date night or going on a couples' retreat. By spending time, looking inwards, you can better position your team to take on the challenges that will inevitably crop up from time to time.

Please bear in mind that teambuilding doesn't always have to be work-centric. Some activities should focus on strengthening your interpersonal relationships. Remember, strong relationships will help you to weather the storms that will inevitably come along.

Identify the Right People

One way to avoid having your meeting participants feel like hostages is to ensure you have the right people in the room. And just how do you determine who are the right people? Well, that depends on your purpose as outlined above.

Based on your role as manager, it's likely that you will hold many of your meetings with your direct reports. However, there are times when you will need to draw on resources from outside your chain of command. For example, in an information-sharing meeting, you many need to call on a colleague or a senior manager to answer questions and provide clarification as required.

If it's a meeting where decisions will be taken, you need to ensure that the people around the table have the legitimate authority, and that the entities they represent have agreed to accept said decisions. Otherwise your entire process could be derailed.

Similarly, for a brainstorming meeting, you may want to secure the services of a facilitator so that you are free to engage in the creative

JOAN H. UNDERWOOD

process, rather than being distracted by the responsibilities associated with managing the meeting. The same principle could apply for some of the more intense team building meetings.

Provide Adequate Notice

One of the most common complaints all up and down the organisational chart is a lack of time. Conflicting priorities probably comes in a close second. Therefore, if you truly want meeting invitees to show up for you, it's absolutely essential you give them adequate notice and confirm their availability.

However, you want people to do more than just show up. You want to ensure that they're optimally prepared. Here again, time is essential—especially in those cases where you're going to rely on attendees to provide information or contribute to decision-making. Therefore, available/relevant background documents should accompany the meeting notice, and it should be made absolutely clear that the meeting will proceed based on the assumption that participants have completed the background readings.

Other critical elements to include in the meeting notice are venue, date and time, duration, meeting format/process, and the agenda, including targeted outcomes. The final element is particularly important to help invitees answer the "what's in it for me?" question.

In the context of the meteoric increase in the use of online platforms occasioned by the Covid-19 pandemic, I should point out that the factors I have just outlined apply equally to virtual meetings. In addition to ensuring you have clearly articulated your purpose, selected the right individuals, and provided adequate notice in advance of the meeting, your preparation for a virtual meeting should include ensuring the selected platform is operational and that meeting participants can readily access it . Therefore, your meeting notice should include this information along with any instructions that your attendees might require to download the software, and ensure that the device they will use to access the meeting complies with the necessary technical specifications.

Establish and Communicate Ground Rules

One school of thought advocates establishing the ground rules at the start of the meeting. However, I maintain that during the meeting is the time for rule enforcement—not rule establishment. Otherwise, you risk having your agenda go sideways as participants debate whether they consider the rule(s) in question acceptable. In fact, depending on the culture within your organisation or the mindset of your stakeholder invitees, you may wish to adopt alternative language and refer to terms of engagement as opposed to rules. Some folks—especially people over whom you have no legitimate authority—may have an almost visceral response to being presented with rules.

Having completed these pre-meeting preparations, it's now time to facilitate your great meeting.

During the Meeting

"Meetings are at the heart of an effective organisation, and each meeting is an opportunity to clarify issues, set new directions, sharpen focus, create alignment, and move objectives forward."
— Paul Axtell[27]

One of the great paradoxes of leadership is that it's not about you, but rather about how you get things done through others. To fulfil the promise reflected in our lead quotation, you must skilfully guide

---

[27] Paul Axtell, *Meetings Matter: 8 Powerful Strategies for Remarkable Conversations*

JOAN H. UNDERWOOD

and direct the process without appearing to dominate it. The meeting is not about the person chairing it. Rather, it's about the agenda and the targeted outcomes as outlined in the previous section. It is important to bear in mind that all parties are present in service to those two items.

Let's turn our attention to five specific steps to take in order to fulfil these obligations and facilitate a great meeting.

Respect the Time

There is a real temptation to delay the start of the meeting until the majority of the participants have arrived. Think about the message that sends to those who made the effort—and even sacrifice—to show up on time. Chances are that they won't make the same effort the next time you convene a meeting.

During my tenure as the HR Manager with a financial conglomerate, I presided over quarterly general staff meetings. It became apparent to me that the organisational culture considered it acceptable to stroll into the meeting room well after the scheduled start time. The habit had been inadvertently reinforced by the practice of providing recaps as tardy staff members joined the meeting.

So, to break the back of that non-productive habit, I made a public announcement that meetings would start on time—as long as there was at least one person present (by the way, the stipulation that one other person be present was to avoid the questionable spectre of my addressing an empty room). I went on to point out that this was my way of rewarding punctuality and conveying respect to those who made the effort to arrive on time. Of course, some folks still arrived late. However, they knew it was their personal responsibility to bring themselves up to speed on what they had missed—and that they could not disrupt the proceedings to do so.

Respecting the time also means adhering to the time allocated for each agenda item and concluding the meeting at the scheduled time. In the event that you note the deliberations are legitimately taking longer than anticipated, the appropriate course of action is to draw the matter to the attendees' attention, and give them the opportunity to have input in the decision about whether to move forward with the agenda or to extend the time. By involving them in the decision-making process, you minimise the risk of having them feel like they're being held hostage.

Engage All Meeting Participants

As the meeting's facilitator, it's your responsibility to ensure everyone present has the opportunity to contribute to the discussion. Some people will need no special invitation, while you will need to draw others out. The caveat here is that you should do this in a positive way and not in a way that appears to be picking on them. This may require the use of softeners, and open-ended questions are definitely more effective. E.g. "Jason, we know that your department has experience implementing similar projects. What are some of the lessons learnt that could be beneficial to us as we take on this new project?"

One of the reasons why it's safe to call on Jason relates to what we covered in a previous section—i.e. ensuring you have the right people in the room and that they have prior knowledge of the matters to be discussed and the specific preparation they needed to complete ahead of the meeting.

Just as you may need to draw some people out, you may need to get some people to relinquish some of the bandwidth—so to speak. Here again, tact and skill are important to minimise the likelihood of their withdrawing completely.

Special word of caution—hold off on expressing your opinion

until you have heard from the attendees. If there is a significant power distance, your early declaration could serve to stymie further discussion. It could also create the impression that you have already made a decision and are just going through the motions in soliciting their input.

Listen Attentively

Most of us have a tendency to listen in order to respond. To facilitate a great meeting, you need to listen to understand. This means that you listen from a place of curiosity, and that you listen both to what is said and what is unsaid. It also means you go beyond using your ears for listening and include your eyes and heart.

Attentive listening will also enable you to use questions as an alternative to declaratory statements as a means of advancing the discussion. It also directs you away from jumping to conclusions, making assumptions, and generally pontificating. Plus you are likely to accumulate bonus points when it becomes apparent that you are genuinely and authentically listening and taking in the contributions being made.

Manage Gender Issues

This section is for all genders, so I hope you won't gloss over it... Be on the lookout for cases of *manterruping* and *bropropriating*. What exactly do I mean by that?

Manterrupting: Unnecessary interruption of a woman by a man. E.g: when Kanye West made his way on the stage to interrupt/disrupt Taylor Swift's acceptance speech during the 2009 MTV Video Music Awards.

Bropropriating: Taking a woman's idea and taking credit for it. Research published by Sheryl Sandberg and Wharton business school professor Adam Grant describes this as follows: "When a woman speaks in a professional setting, she walks a tightrope. Either she's barely heard or she's judged as too aggressive. When a man says virtually the same thing, heads nod in appreciation for his fine idea."[28]

Those who know better should do better. So, now that these two counterproductive gender-related meeting practices have been flagged, I encourage you to wage a campaign to eliminate them from your meetings (or prevent them from starting).

Use a Parking Lot

Many potentially great meetings get derailed by important yet non-relevant discussions. As the guardian of the process, it's your responsibility to defer such discussions to a more suitable time and forum. You would have set the foundation for this by clearly identifying the meeting purpose when you sent out the agenda. Therefore, when such matters are raised, you should not hesitate to tactfully refer participants to the purpose as presented in the agenda, even as you acknowledge the importance of the item that has been raised. The caveat here is that you simply must remember to honour your commitment to have the issue addressed—or referred to the appropriate parties—at a subsequent time. Failure to do so could have an adverse impact on your personal credibility.

Capture and Recap Decisions and Action Items

You already know you need to have your agenda before you to facilitate a great meeting. As decisions are made, go ahead and record them alongside the relevant agenda item. Your notes should also include task owners, timelines for completion, and quality standards. This helps to clarify what constitutes satisfactory completion. By

---

[28] https://time.com/3666135/sheryl-sandberg-talking-while-female-manterruptions/

JOAN H. UNDERWOOD

getting into this level of detail, you increase the likelihood that the actions taken will optimally align with your original purpose/intent.

By reviewing the decisions and action items prior to concluding the meeting, you help participants to operate from a shared pool of understanding. It also provides an opportunity for task owners to seek any required clarification.

Finally, it's a good idea to circulate a summary of decisions and action items to all meeting participants within a day or two of the meeting—while the discussions are still fresh in their minds. Receiving that email will also serve as a reminder for people to get started on implementation.

After the Meeting

"Many people don't focus enough on execution. If you make a commitment to get something done, you need to follow through on that commitment."
—Kenneth Chenault[xxx]

In the two previous sections, you learnt how to prepare for and facilitate a great meeting. Now the meeting is over, and it's time for the real work to begin. You see, what really determines if your meeting was truly great is whether you and the other participants follow up and follow through. We've probably all been to meetings which went quite well, only to discover that all the great talk never translated into great action. So let's explore some ways to ensure your meetings don't suffer the same fate.

Evaluate Extent to Which Meeting Fulfilled Purpose

Once the meeting has concluded, in your role as convener, you should take time out to assess the extent to which the stipulated purpose has been achieved. The following grid presents a useful qualitative rating.

Type of Meeting Result	Low Impact	Medium Impact	High Impact
Information Shared Transfer knowledge to advance the work	Provide status reports or educational presentations	Discuss potential relevance of knowledge transfer	Identify implications from knowledge transfer and use to advance the work
Problem Solved Overcome obstacles to advance the work	Identify causes and brainstorm ideas to address them	Evaluate ideas and develop robust recommendations for solving them	Make commitments to implement selected solutions
Strategy/Action Plan Developed	Identify potential activities	Define desired outcomes/results and key steps to get there	Sequence and schedule actions; identify any critical path dependencies
Commitments to Action Concretised	Say who will do what	Say who will do what and by when	Say who will do what, by when, and set quality expectations

Prepare Meeting Summary and Action List

Utilising your notes from the meeting, prepare a summary of decisions taken as well as the list of action items and disseminate to all meeting attendees within 48 hours of the meeting. As mentioned in the previous section, receipt of the summary will serve as a reminder for task owners to initiate action on their deliverables.

That list should include the following information:

- Actions to be taken/tasks to be completed
- Task owner
- Supporting parties/resources
- Due date

- Quality standards
- Reporting requirements

Hold Yourself and Others Accountable

Accountability is the ability to make commitments to action, then keep those commitments, or acknowledge that you haven't and figure out what you need to do to move to action. Your responsibility doesn't end once you've sent out the meeting summary and action items. Without micromanaging the process, you should follow up to ensure task owners are making the necessary progress.

It is important to take into consideration the fact that, based on their past experiences, people may perceive the accountability conversation as a negative experience, accusatory, punishment, or an implicit indication of a lack of confidence in their ability. One tool that could assist you in holding people accountable without raising their ire is the Accountability Ladder, which I introduced in Chapter 5.

Once you have established a team culture which stipulates that everyone is required to operate on the upper rungs of the ladder,[29] then you would have laid the foundation for holding people accountable for delivering on assigned duties and responsibilities. In such a culture, it is perfectly clear there is zero tolerance for behaviour associated with the lower rungs of the accountability ladder—behaviours such as blaming others, making excuses, or adopting a wait-and-hope approach as the default strategy for resolving problems.

Follow-up—Find the Sweet Spot

When it comes to follow-up, the goal is to find the sweet spot between abdicating responsibility and micromanaging. Once you've prepared

---

[29] When operating on the upper rungs of the Accountability Ladder, individuals acknowledge and own reality, find solutions, and fix problems.

and confirmed the plan of action including task owners, reporting schedules, required support/resources, and due dates, you've laid the foundation for your participants to execute. However, that doesn't mean you can sit back and assume that cruise control will get you to the desired destination. Rather, what is required is vigilance and a light touch on the steering wheel/controls to adjust as required based on any course deviations resulting from unforeseen circumstances. This light-touch follow-up also sends a clear signal to your colleagues that their contribution is important and that you're committed to supporting them in a way that is free of judgment, yet fully committed to the desired outcomes.

 ## Application Exercise: Plan and Facilitate a Great Meeting

You now know everything you need to know to convene your first great meeting. So, it's time to create an action plan and then put that plan in motion.

1. Determine the type of meeting you will be convening.
   A. Information sharing
   B. Decision making
   C. Problem solving
   D. Innovation/brainstorming
   E. Team building
2. Identify the objective of your meeting.
3. Based on the objective, determine who needs to be present.
4. Select an appropriate date, time, and venue for the meeting.
5. Prepare and disseminate the meeting notice. Remember to include the following:

A. Date, time, venue, duration (and login instructions if it's an online meeting)
B. Agenda
C. Ground rules/terms of engagement
D. Targeted outcome
E. Any required advance preparation
F. RSVP information
6. Make arrangements for someone to take notes at the meeting
7. Convene your meeting
8. Remember—take no hostages!
9. Send out a meeting summary within 48 hours
10. Follow up to ensure that the decisions taken are implemented

CHAPTER EIGHTEEN

BANISHING THE MYTH OF TIME MANAGEMENT

*"There are no time management problems. There
are only priority management problems."*
–JohnMichaelMorgan.com

I HAD NO INTENTION OF WRITING THIS CHAPTER, BUT MY MARKET research revealed that my target audience thought that time management was an important topic. So this chapter is my way of writing about time management while holding firm to my belief that it's not a real thing.

The Cambridge Dictionary defines management as the control and organisation of something. So, while I can control and organise many things—e.g. my career, my company, my money—I have zero control over time. And when it comes to its organisation, it is what it is. There are sixty minutes in an hour; twenty-four hours in a day; seven days in a week—you get the idea. Time is a finite resource. I can't make more of it, and I can't reorganise it into some other configuration. What I do have control over is what I do with the time available to me—and everyone else for that matter. And what I can organise is my approach to how I spend the time.

The Importance of Setting Priorities

The key is not to prioritise what's on your schedule but to schedule your priorities.

There's a story that has been making the rounds for so many years that I wonder if it's an urban myth. Whether it's real or not, there's a reason for its longevity. That's why I've opted to share with you the story of "The Rocks, Pebbles, and Sand."

A philosophy professor once stood before his class with a large empty jar. He filled the jar with large rocks and asked his students if the jar was full. The students said that, yes, the jar was full.

He then added small pebbles to the jar and asked again, "Is the jar full now?" The students agreed that the jar was indeed full.

The professor then poured sand into the jar and asked again. The students then agreed that the jar was finally full.

The professor went on to explain that the jar signifies one's life. The rocks are equivalent to the most important things in your life, such as family, health, and relationships. And if the pebbles and the sand were lost, the jar would still be full, and your life would still have a meaning.

The pebbles represent the other things that matter in your life, such as your work, school, and house. These things often come and go and are not permanent or essential to your overall wellbeing.

And finally, the sand represents the remaining small stuff and material possessions in your life. These things don't mean much to your life as a whole and are likely only done to waste time or get small tasks accomplished.

This story is a metaphor highlighting the importance of prioritizing. When you choose to take care of the big things first, you then find that you have the space and time to fit in the smaller things.

Contrast the approach recommended by the professor to one where you simply tackle things that appear on your to-do list in the order in which they got added to it. For most people, that list gets made as things pop into their heads or as someone makes a request. The problem with that approach is that there is no context, no mindfulness, no prioritization. The approach is also incongruent with one of my mantras when it comes to work—i.e. begin with the end in mind.

Whenever I'm approached about taking on a new assignment, I ask myself whether it aligns with my purpose, or one of the goals that cascade down from my purpose. That's the first hurdle that needs to be crossed. Once it satisfies that criterion, I then consider whether I have the bandwidth to take it on. In doing so, I typically explore whether there are synergies with anything I'm already doing so that I might reduce the incremental effort required. As a result of this process, by the time something makes it onto my to-do list, it has context and alignment. It also has a due date and level of importance attached to it.

So how does this translate for you as you embrace your role as a new manager? For the purpose of this discussion, let's restrict the universe of time to your work hours. In that way, I'm not asking you to make judgment calls about your work-life balance. Rather, let's focus on how you choose to spend you work week—however long that is. The answer to that question is determined by the priorities you establish. Complete the following exercise to identify your big rocks.

Application Exercise: Establish Your Schedule Based on Your Priorities

1. Establish your team's purpose. Note well that I didn't ask you to establish your personal purpose. That's because as a manager, you are responsible for your team. You are no longer just an individual contributor.[30]

2. In order for you to fulfil that purpose, what are the four or so things you need to focus on? These are your strategic priorities.

    Example: Some years ago, I went through this exercise with a CEO I was coaching. Her board had mandated the coaching intervention to support her professional development and to help her overcome her tendency to "major in the minor." She completed this step by identifying the following strategic priorities:

    *   Execute Board Directives
    *   Design and implement strategic interventions
    *   Execute calendar events/stakeholder engagement activities

3. Cross-reference the strategic priorities that you have identified with your job description. Are you able to align each of your core responsibilities with a strategic priority? If not, you should consider whether you need to revisit your list of strategic priorities. If you determine that the item in question does not rise to the level of a strategic priority, then designate it as either a pebble or sand, which you will add to your jar later—after you've put in the big rocks.

---

[30] You can refer to the team charter you prepared in Chapter 15 rather than coming up with a new answer.

4. For each strategic priority, determine what your goals are for the year. Write them down along with their respective due dates.

5. Starting from the targeted completion date for each of your goals, work backwards and fill in milestone accomplishments and dates for same.

6. Make a list of the action items you need to complete to roll up into your goals and ultimately your strategic priorities. These are your rocks. Put them in the jar by entering them in your calendar/schedule.

7. Double check you have allocated time each week to work on each of your strategic priorities.

8. Having secured the space in your schedule for the big rocks, you should then block out time to deal with the pebbles and sand. These are the activities that do not rise to the level of a strategic priority, but which require your time and attention.

Differentiating between Urgent and Important

So many managers spend the majority of their days putting out fires. They lurch from one thing to another at a frenetic pace, because everything has taken on the semblance of urgency. The thing is, there's a difference between being urgent and being important. The two don't necessarily go together.

For sure, the big rocks you identified in the preceding exercise are definitely important. If you don't take care of them in a timely manner as per the schedule you just created, a time will come when they are both important and urgent. The pebbles and sand don't rise to the same level of importance as the big rocks. However, if you don't pay attention to them, they can become urgent—i.e. they require immediate attention. If that is the norm, rather than the exception, you run the risk of having them displace the big rocks.

Here's another metaphor that might help to bring the point home. Putting batteries in your smoke detectors could be considered as a pebble. However, if you never get around to it, and there's a fire in the house, the situation becomes urgent. What could have been prevented or at least minimised/mitigated now takes on a life of its own and demands immediate and focused attention, ultimately taking precedence over everything else you were planning to do.

The takeaway from making the distinction between urgent and important is to focus on taking care of both the rocks and the pebbles in a timely and consistent manner, so that you can focus on being an effective manager rather than an amateur firefighter.

God Rested, and So Should You

In your enthusiasm to excel in your new role, you might be tempted to burn your candle at both ends, to be the first to arrive and the last one to leave. The truth is that there are days when that's what you will be required to do. However, if you find that it's the norm rather than the exception, then something is definitely wrong.

Your role as a manager is not meant to consume your life. As we discovered in Chapter 7, you can't pour from an empty cup, and self-care cannot be delegated. However, those aren't the only reasons why you shouldn't always be the first to arrive at the office in the mornings and the last to leave at night. The truth is that that pattern of behaviour is likely to raise concerns that you are out of your depth, and that you're struggling to keep up with the requirements of the job. It could cause your employer to wonder if you have the capacity to get the job done without burning out.

In addition to raising questions in your boss's mind, habitually burning the candle at both ends sends a message to your direct reports. As a manager, you cast a long shadow. Your behaviour essentially serves as an example to emulate. In response, some members of your team might feel guilty for leaving work on time. Others may stay longer but resent you for making them feel that they have to do so. And to round out the lose-lose-lose scenario, your peers might feel that you're trying to show them up.

As I said at the beginning of this chapter, I don't believe that time management is a real thing. However, I understand you might feel overwhelmed by what you need to get done and the limited time that's available to do it. As I've pointed out, it's all about assigning priorities and making choices. There's one more thing that I'd like to add at this point, and that's the importance of setting boundaries.

You have more than one role in your life. Being a manager is one of many roles. You may also be a son/daughter, a mother/father, a spouse, a best friend, a niece/nephew. Someone is counting on you in each and every one of those roles. It's not prudent or desirable to make a habit out of short-changing them. At the end of the day, being a manager is your job—it's not your life. Throughout this book, I've provided guidance to help you be the best manager you could possibly be. I also wish for you to be the best human that you can be. For this reason, I share with you two biblical passages which put work in its proper context.

Our labour is to be a blessing for us—not a worry.
[Ecclesiastes 5:12]

&

It is useless for you to work so hard from early
morning to late at night, anxiously working for food
to eat; for God gives rest to His loved ones.
[Psalm 127:2]

JOAN H. UNDERWOOD

The Art of Saying No

"A NO uttered from deepest conviction is better and greater than a YES merely uttered to please, or what is worse, to avoid trouble."
—Gandhi

In order for you to achieve and maintain balance between your roles in life, there's one final skill I wish to share with you—the art of saying no. It takes practice to say no and not feel guilty about it, or not be consumed with worry that your refusal has done irreparable damage to the relationship or your job prospects. I guarantee you that it's worth it to put in the necessary practice. On the other side of the hard work is a degree of liberation that will enable you to reclaim time that would otherwise be lost to you.

Just to be clear, there are some low- or no-risk situations where it's easy to say no. You're probably already handling those situations well all on your own. You don't need any guidance from me there. However, the stakes are higher when you need to say no to a boss, a client, a peer, or even a direct report, and you think that your no may not be well received. Here are some tips to help you navigate those tight spots.

Tip #1: According to Holly Weeks,[xxxi] one option is to aim for a neutral demeanour such as you would expect from a referee in a game. A ref makes a call, regardless of strong feelings on both sides. His job is to give his decision and stay with it if challenged. A neutral no is delivered without hesitation, emotion, or apology. It is decisive without being harsh.

If your no is challenged, again, follow the example of the referee—stick to your guns. If you know you made the right call, then don't vacillate. That doesn't mean you can't acknowledge the other person's disappointment. What it does mean is that you don't let that disappointment overshadow the valid reasons you had for saying no in the first place. This approach might come in handy with a client who is asking you to bend the rules in a way that represents a slippery slope that could compromise you or your organisation.

Tip #2 is to suggest an alternative. Depending on the situation, that could mean suggesting another time when you can do what is being asked of you, or it could mean recommending someone else to perform the task. I utilise this strategy quite often in my consulting practice. Sometimes I get requests to do an assignment when I don't have the bandwidth (based on having prioritised other work). In such cases, I thank the individual for considering me for the job and explain that I have limited availability, but would be willing to suggest one or two other people who might be better positioned to assist at that time.

When you use this type of no, you have some follow-up work to do. Get in touch with the people you recommended to give them a heads up. It's also a good idea for you to follow up with the person making the request to inquire whether they got the help they needed. Please note that this is not meant to open the door for them to try to strong arm you into taking on the task. Therefore, I recommend that you let some time pass before you make that follow-up call. And when you do, place the call in the context of valuing the relationship and the confidence that they have in you, and reaffirm that you would be more than happy to collaborate with them in the future when your schedule is more open.

Tip #3: Frame your no as a counterproposal. So, for example, if someone asks you to do something at a time when you are scheduled to work on one of your big rocks, and you need to maintain that schedule so that it doesn't end up becoming a fire you have to put out, you

JOAN H. UNDERWOOD

could say something along these lines: "I appreciate your asking for my help. I have an important prior commitment that I can't reschedule. However, if it works for you, I'd be happy to give you a hand at such and such a time... Would that work for you?"

Tip #4: If it's your boss who is making the request, then you might really feel pressured to say yes and then burn the midnight oil to deliver what they asked as well as what you were originally scheduled to do. All that time, you will probably feel like a martyr—or something worse. Here's something that has worked really well for me—tell them what you have scheduled and then ask if they would like you to defer working on that and to focus on the new request instead. I can't tell you how many times the response in such situations has been, "No, what you're working on takes precedence over this. I'll get someone else to take care of it."

And there you have it—my chapter on time management that really isn't about managing time at all, but rather about managing your choices, particularly the choice of how you spend your time.

I can think of no better way to end this chapter and this book other than commending you for choosing to spend this time equipping yourself with the knowledge, skills, and abilities to more effectively manage yourself, manage others, and manage systems and processes.

PART IV
EPILOGUE

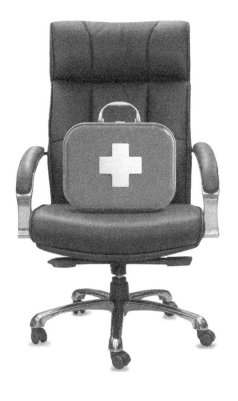

EVERY WINNER WAS
ONCE A BEGINNER

E VERY WINNER WAS ONCE A BEGINNER. THIS IS IMPORTANT TO BEAR in mind when starting any endeavour—including your journey to becoming an incredible manager. Sometimes success seems immediately within our grasp when we set out towards a goal. However, far more often, the path to success is difficult and sometimes unclear. We don't know if or how we will succeed. And that's okay. When you start a challenge, you don't necessarily need to have the blueprint to success. What's more important in that initial phase is the will to succeed and the determination to persist—even when you stumble, even when you fall and struggle to get back up.

Every winner was once a beginner—a beginner with a vision and with the determination to succeed. It is that vision and the determination to attain it that keeps you going when it would be so easy to stop. That's why it's so important to begin with the end in mind—to visualise your success. What will it look like? What will it feel like? In addition to you, who else will benefit from or revel in your success?

If you have not already done so, visualise yourself as a successful, high-performing manager—one who is trusted and respected by your direct reports, trusted and admired by your peers, and trusted and relied upon by your boss. Create a vivid, detailed image. Flesh out the details—where are you when your success is being celebrated or acknowledged? What are you wearing? Who else is present? What are they wearing? Picture faces… how would you describe the look on your face? On their faces? Are you sitting/standing/walking/running? See it all. Look at it the way you would look at a painting or a movie playing out on a big screen. Absorb everything unfolding before you.

Once you've taken in every detail of the image of success, I invite you to step into it—I mean that literally. Instead of looking at yourself in your moment of success, step into yourself. Become part of the portrait or movie before you and then take a moment to see what it feels like. You are no longer in the present moment—rather, you have been transported into your future self at the moment when you're celebrating your win. What does it feel like—physically? Emotionally? Let the feelings permeate your being. Savour them. Cherish them. Give yourself a mental high five in acknowledgment of the fact that you've transitioned from a beginner to a winner. Stay in that moment as long as you want to… as long as you need to… Return to the present moment only when you're ready.

Once you've returned to the present moment, I invite you to make a promise to yourself. Whenever you're feeling tired/frustrated/doubtful/afraid/concerned that you didn't handle a particular situation in the best way possible, and disappointed that you didn't apply the lessons you learnt in this book, I encourage you to repeat this visualisation exercise. Don't just remember it. Rather, see it and then step into it. Immerse yourself in it once again and allow yourself to experience the jubilation, the joy, the pride, and every other emotion that you just experienced. Do this as often as you need to in order to persevere until you win.

As you pursue your goal of becoming an exceptional manager, think of yourself as an athlete preparing for the Olympics. Keep your eye and your heart on the prize. Today, you might be a beginner or someone who has stumbled. If you make the commitment to persevere, the day will come when you are no longer a beginner, but a winner!

AUTHOR BIO

JOAN H. UNDERWOOD IS THE MANAGING DIRECTOR OF UNDERWOOD Talent Development Services (UTDS), an acclaimed consulting firm specializing in helping professionals, business enterprises, governments, and Caribbean institutions develop high-performance individuals, teams, and strategies. Joan holds a Masters in Health Services Administration from the George Washington University and an Executive MBA from the Cave Hill School of Business/University of the West Indies. Her proverbial tool kit is also equipped with the designations of **Senior Professional in Human Resources** (SPHR), **Accredited Director** (Acc.Dir.) **Master Trainer, Certified Change Practitioner**, and **Erickson Professional Coach.**

With over 20 years as a pioneer in the Caribbean talent development and human resources professions, she was one of twenty-seven outstanding women leaders in the Commonwealth featured in the book *Championing Women Leaders—Beyond Sponsorship.* In addition to her work in coaching, management and policy, Joan served for seven and a half years as Antigua and Barbuda's Non-Resident Ambassador to a number of Latin American countries, including Mexico, Venezuela, Chile, and Brazil.

An avid reader, Joan particularly enjoys a good book, date nights with her husband, Rudie, listening to the sweet melodies of steelband music, fellowship with her church community, and being an active member of the Human Resource Management Association of Barbados (HRMAB).

To learn more about Joan and the range of services offered by UTDS, visit www.utdsinc.com or email info@utdsinc.com.

ENDNOTES

i   Two assessments I highly recommend are the EQ-I 2.0 and the Myers Briggs Type Indicator. Optimally, both should be administered by certified practitioners. However, open source quick-versions can also be found online.

ii   This case was developed as a project for the CAPAM Network of Public Service Training and Development Institutes in partnership with the Governance and Institutional Development Division (GIDD), Commonwealth Secretariat.

iii   Susan David is a founder of the Harvard/McLean Institute of Coaching, is on faculty at Harvard Medical School, and is recognised as one of the world's leading management thinkers. She is author of the #1 *Wall Street Journal* bestseller *Emotional Agility* (Avery) based on the concept named by HBR as a Management Idea of the Year.

iv   John Keyser is the founder and principal of Common Sense Leadership.

v   Based on his experiences in Nazi death camps—including Auschwitz—from 1942 to 1945, Frankl's timeless memoir and meditation on finding meaning in the midst of suffering argues that man cannot avoid suffering but can choose how to cope with it, find meaning in it, and move forward with renewed purpose.

vi   Julie Dirksen is an independent consultant and instructional designer. Her focus has been on utilising the disciplines of educational psychology, neuroscience, change management, and persuasive technology to promote and support the improvement of peoples' lives through sustainable long-term learning and behavioural change.

vii   James Clear is a writer and speaker focused on habits, decision-making, and continuous improvement. He is the author of the New York Times bestseller, *Atomic Habits*. His work has appeared in Entrepreneur magazine, Time magazine, the New York Times, and the Wall Street Journal.

viii   Elizabeth Kubler-Ross is a Swizz-American psychologist who is best known for her pioneering work in near-death studies, and as the author of the internationally bestselling book, *On Death and Dying*.

ix   Kristin Armstrong is a former professional road bicycle racer and three-time Olympic gold medallist, the winner of the women's individual time trial in 2008, 2012, and 2016.

x   Paula Lawes is the author of "A Freedom of Less," in which she describes how having next to nothing can give new meaning to your life.

xi   Matt Haig was born in Sheffield, England in 1975. He writes books for both adults and children, often blending the worlds of domestic reality and outright fantasy, with a quirky twist. His bestselling novels are translated into 28 languages. *The Guardian* has described his writing as 'delightfully weird' and the *New York Times* has called him 'a novelist of great talent' whose writing is 'funny, riveting, and heartbreaking'.

xii   Parker J. Palmer (Madison, WI) is a writer, teacher, and activist whose work speaks deeply to people in many walks of life. Author of eight books—including the bestsellers *Courage to Teach*, *Let Your Life Speak*, and *A Hidden Wholeness*—his writing has been recognised with ten honorary doctorates and many national awards, including the 2010 William Rainey Harper Award (previously won by Margaret Mead, Paulo Freire, and Elie Wiesel). He is founder and senior partner of the Center for Courage Renewal, and holds a Ph.D. from the University of California at Berkeley.

xiii   Paul J. Zak is the founding director of the Center for Neuroeconomics Studies and a professor of economics, psychology, and management at Claremont Graduate University. He is the author of *Trust Factor: The Science of Creating High-Performance Companies* (AMACOM, 2017).

xiv   *ibid*

xv   Ubuntu is an ethic or humanist philosophy focusing on people's allegiances and relations with each other. The word has its origin in the Bantu languages of southern Africa. Ubuntu is seen as a classical African concept.

xvi   Simon may be best known for popularizing the concept of WHY, which he described in his first TED Talk in 2009. That talk went on to become the second most watched TED Talk of all time, and is still in the top five with nearly 50 million views.

xvii   Alan Stein, Jr. teaches proven strategies to improve organisational performance, create effective leadership, increase team cohesion and collaboration, and develop winning mindsets, rituals, and routines. A successful business owner and veteran basketball performance coach, he spent 15 years working with the highest-performing athletes on the planet (including NBA superstars Kevin Durant, Stephen Curry, and Kobe Bryant). In his corporate keynote programs and workshops, Alan reveals how to utilise the same approaches in business that elite athletes use to perform at a world-class level. He delivers practical lessons that can be implemented immediately.

xviii   Warren Gamaliel Bennis is an American scholar, organisational consultant, and author, widely regarded as a pioneer of the contemporary field of Leadership Studies. Bennis is University Professor and Distinguished Professor of Business Administration and Founding Chairman of The Leadership Institute at the University of Southern California.

xix   Dr. Cialdini is known globally as the foundational expert in the science of influence and how to apply it ethically in business. His *Six Principles of Persuasion* have become a cornerstone for any organisation serious about effectively increasing their influence.

xx   Robert Sutton is Professor of Management Science and Engineering at Stanford and a Professor of Organizational Behaviour, by courtesy, at the Stanford Graduate School of Business. Sutton studies innovation, leaders and bosses, evidence-based management, the links between knowledge and organisational action, and workplace civility. This quotation is taken from his book *Good Boss, Bad Boss: How to Be the Best… and Learn from the Worst.*

xxi   In this book, authors Steven Kumble and Kevin Lahart provide an inside account of the rise and fall of the controversial law firm. They describe Finley, Kumble's rapid success and the avarice, betrayal, shady business practices, and feuds that brought about its slide into bankruptcy.

xxii   Monica Wofford is a leadership development expert. She is the author of *Contagious Leadership* and *Make Difficult People Disappear* and works with managers and leaders worldwide, on the prevention of promotion without preparation.

xxiii   Tony Dovale is a South African expert speaker who specialises in *inter alia* high-performance business leadership.

xxiv Simon Sinek (1973) is a leadership guru, professor at Columbia University, founder of SinekPartners (Corporate Refocusing), and author. He is best known for popularizing the concept of "the golden circle" and to "Start With Why". Simon Sinek is also an adjunct staff member of the RAND Corporation.

xxv Patrick Lencioni is founder and president of The Table Group, a firm dedicated to providing organisations with ideas, products, and services that improve teamwork, clarity, and employee engagement. He is the author of *The Five Dysfunctions of a Team*, which remains a fixture on national bestseller lists.

xxvi Malicious compliance is so common in today's workplace that it has its own community of almost one million members on reddit. You can check it out for some cautionary tales as well as some hilarious stories.

xxvii Peter Clay Carroll is an American football coach who is the head coach and executive vice president of the Seattle Seahawks of the National Football League. He is also the founder of Compete to Create, a high-performance training company headquartered in Seattle.

xxviii Of his five books on leadership, coaching, and sports, *Coaching for Performance* is the best known, having sold over a million copies in more than 20 languages. This seminal text introduced the world to the GROW Model, created by Sir John and his colleagues in the 1980s.

xxix Michael is founder and Managing Director for Leadership Strategies (www.leadstrat.com).

xxx Kenneth Irvine Chenault is an American business executive. He was the CEO and Chairman of American Express from 2001 until 2018. He is the third African American CEO of a Fortune 500 company.

xxxi Holly Weeks publishes, teaches, and consults on communications issues. She is Adjunct Lecturer in Public Policy at the Harvard Kennedy School, and the author of *Failure to Communicate: How Conversations Go Wrong and What You Can Do to Right Them* (Harvard Business School Press, 2008).